AHDOOLO!

AHDOOLO!

THE BIOGRAPHY OF

MATTHEW A. HENSON

by Floyd Miller

E. P. DUTTON & CO., INC.

NEW YORK · 1963

Published simultaneously in Canada by
Clarke, Irwin & Company Limited,
Toronto and Vancouver

Portions of this book first appeared in the
February 1963 issue of *The Reader's Digest*

Library of Congress Catalog Card Number: 63–15771

For Frank Kolars

Illustrations

Acknowledgments

I first came upon the legend of Matthew Henson through a visit with Admiral Donald MacMillan. Sitting in his Provincetown home (which is as much museum as house), this last survivor of the Peary 1909 expedition to the North Pole told weird and wonderful stories that brought his old comrade to life. From that day this book was destined. MacMillan is in no way responsible for the conclusions reached on the following pages, but he is responsible for the beginning of my outrage that history should have largely passed over such a man as Henson.

As I began my research on this biography I was amazed to find the high degree of emotion that exists today over events of five decades ago. In 1909 both Commander Robert E. Peary and Dr. Frederick Cook claimed to have discovered the North Pole, and there was launched a public controversy seldom matched for acrimony. Even today the descendants of these two families are touched by the original passion. Historians and biographers who have treated this material have, in general, become partisans. Such was the high adventure, the heroism, the suffering and stunning disappointments, the betrayals and perfidy surrounding these two that no man could view them without being moved.

It was the very intensity of the battle that seemed to obscure the fact that a third man was most intimately involved. In truth, if there had not been this third man, this quiet Negro named Matthew Henson, there would have been no controversy; there would have been no discovery of the Pole—at least, not in that day by that cast of men. This book, then, is about that catalyst—Matthew Henson.

After being alerted to this story by Admiral MacMillan, I went to see Marie Peary Stafford, the famous "Snow Baby" who was born in the North during her father's second North Greenland Expedition. Today she is the keeper of the Peary archives, the gallant defender of the Peary name. When I presented myself to her in Brunswick, Maine, she told me, with traditional family bluntness, that she heartily disapproved of my project. Yet, such was her graciousness and sense of fair play that she gave me her attention, then her memories, and finally access to the Peary files.

No less gallant was Cook's daughter, Helene Cook Vetter. Knowing I had become convinced that the truth was mainly on Peary's side, she still went to considerable trouble to supply me with material concerning Henson.

Lucy Henson, Matthew's widow, living in the pin-neat Harlem apartment she shared with her husband, gave me scrapbooks that were of great value. Herbert Frisby, reporter for the *Baltimore Afro-American*, exposed me to his extraordinary energy and record of accomplishment on behalf of Henson's memory.

Dr. Vilhjalmur Stefansson received me at Hanover, New Hampshire, about a month before his death. In his eighties, he was lucid and incisive and uncompromising. The intellectual among Arctic explorers, he pungently put the period and its men in perspective and urged the completion of this book. H. Wales Lee, son of Peary's companion on the Greenland ice cap, let me read his father's unpublished diary with its moving accounts of suffering and heroism. My friend, Professor Kenneth Wiggins of the City College of New York and of Block Island, kindly read the manuscript to check my geography and celestial navigation.

Librarians are surely a special breed. Their enthusiasm and enterprise have sustained many a writer. I am particularly indebted to the following: Evelyn Stefansson, Baker Library, Dartmouth College; Frederick Meigs, Main Navy Library, Washington, D.C.; Ona Lee McKeen, Library of Congress, Washington, D.C.; Vir-

ginia Hills, National Geographical Society, Washington, D.C.;
Virginia Richardson, Morgan State College, Baltimore, Maryland;
Katherine Zimmerman, historian, Bureau of Yards and Docks,
United States Navy, Arlington, Virginia; and my own librarians
in Nyack, New York, Mary Proper and Edith Doig.

AHDOOLO!

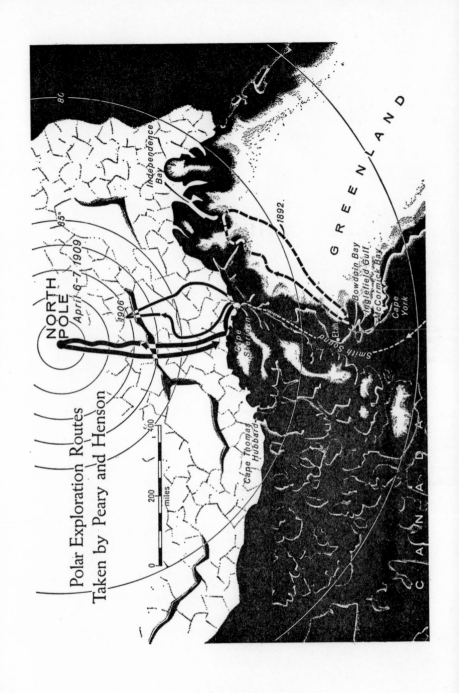

Polar Exploration Routes Taken by Peary and Henson

[I]

On "G" Street in Washington, D.C., stood the hat store of B. H. Steinmetz and Sons, and it seemed an unlikely starting point for great events. It was filled with a musty-dusty odor, and generally with a quiet that was neither repose nor contemplation, but merely a vacuum awaiting the entrance of a customer. Moreover, the very merchandise tended to depress the spirit: rack upon rack of identical brims and crowns gave the illusion of a battalion of faceless creatures pressed into ultimate conformity.

And yet a man's destiny, if it is bold enough and strong enough, can overtake him most any place. It overtook Matthew Henson in the spring of 1887. He was stock boy in that hat store.

"Matt!" called Sam Steinmetz from the display room. "Bring a size seven and three-eighths sun helmet. They're on the shelf above the panamas."

Henson moved a small stepladder, ran up it with twenty-year-old nonchalance, retrieved an oval hatbox, and jumped down to carry it quickly to the front room. There both his employer and the customer looked at him in a speculative manner.

"This is the boy I was telling you about, Lieutenant," Steinmetz said.

The customer was a young naval officer, tall and spare, yet

deep of chest. His sandy hair and shaggy mustache framed a strong, aquiline nose and blue eyes that were measuring but without craft. His impeccable manners did not, however, entirely cover a thrust of steel—the metal of his ambition and his absolute self-control.

He accepted the sun helmet, adjusted it levelly on his head, looked into the mirror, and said to Henson's reflection, "I am Lieutenant Peary, and I'm going to Nicaragua to survey a proposed ship's canal between the Atlantic and Pacific Oceans. I need a responsible boy to go with me as personal servant, to keep my clothes and quarters clean. It's jungle country, a nasty climate; the work won't be easy. Mr. Steinmetz recommends you. Do you want the job?"

Unperturbed by the lieutenant's abruptness, Henson thought a moment, then said, "Yes, sir, I think I'd like to have it."

Peary removed the sun helmet, indicated he would take it, then demanded of the boy, "What other jobs have you had?"

Henson was a Negro and his jobs had all been modest ones. He told his story in a soft, unaccented voice with a straightforward regard for facts. He neither boasted nor apologized. He was shorter than the lieutenant, and stockier, but his brown skin covered flat, hard muscles that moved his body with beautiful coordination. He had that combination of strength and grace which promised an easy mastery of any manual skill. When he finished his story he stopped talking.

The officer studied him a moment longer, observed a quiet dignity quite remarkable in one so young, and finally said, "I will supply you transportation, all maintenance, and pay you twenty dollars a month. If that is satisfactory, be prepared to leave within two weeks."

These crisp, commonplace words established a relationship that was to be unique. Lieutenant Peary was to become Admiral Robert E. Peary, the relentless explorer of the Arctic, finally the discoverer of the North Pole, and Matthew Henson was to be with him from 1887 to 1909, a twenty-two-year journey. They were to be bound together with the intimacy of loneliness, of pain, of hunger, of defeat. They were together, half alive, at the moment of triumph.

Ten days following the sale of the sun helmet, Matthew Henson received an envelope containing a railroad ticket for one passage from Washington to New York, and additional cash to take him to a designated pier on the Brooklyn waterfront where he was to meet Peary on board a steamer. He had no one to say good-by to, except Sam Steinmetz, and his total possessions fitted on his back and into a small cardboard case. He walked under the great arches of the Washington railroad terminal, took a faded green plush seat in the rear of the smoking car, all with an inconspicuousness bordering on the invisible. Even the conductor who took his ticket failed to see him, and was aware only that a brown hand held out the proper pasteboard. No one could have known that this man was to become a legend in his time, a folk hero among the Eskimos; that he was to be propelled into the bitter controversy between Peary and Cook, hooted and jeered in public; and in the end was to receive a medal from a Congress reluctant and dismayed at the necessity of honoring a "nigger" but bowing to public opinion. None of this attention, this notoriety, was sought by Henson. What drove him was a thirst for adventure; the rest was a by-product of his time and his color.

When Henson arrived in Brooklyn and found the ship that was to take him to Nicaragua the decks were a scene of confusion. Not only was baggage and equipment and ship's stores being taken aboard, but the large party of civil engineers milled aimlessly about. They were mustachioed men in whipcord pants and puttees, and their broad gestures and loud words were designed to cover the fact that most of them had never before been aboard a ship.

Henson walked among them with a light, sure step, and disappeared below. He had never been aboard this particular ship before, yet he knew his way about. The truth was, he was an Able Seaman. He had first shipped out when he was twelve years old.

The year was 1879 when a ragged Negro boy came to the Baltimore waterfront and stared, open-mouthed, at the towering ships. None of them seemed more glorious than the three-masted sail and steam merchantman *Katie Hines*. Her shrouds ran to crosstrees at a dizzying height, and her name was carved on her bow in letters as high as Matthew himself, and were surely made of pure gold.

A hulking man of sixty years looked down at him from the port rail. His hair was white and his face and hands the color of teakwood and his voice could carry to the topgallants from the weather deck in the middle of a nor'easter. He was Captain Childs and he was as impressive as his ship.

Captain Childs knew men; he had to in order to select a proper crew in these boisterous days. He could look at a man and tell the difference between courage and bravado, between silence and sullenness, between shyness and fear, and he could handle each condition with quick justice. He was able to run his ship with a relaxed hand because his men knew he was capable of righteous violence.

He looked down now at the colored boy and knew the boy wanted to speak to him. But he gave him no help; he merely looked and waited.

Matthew swallowed several times, then called, "You the captain, sir?"

"Aye," boomed Childs.

Again a moment of silence while the boy worked up to the next sentence. "You need a cabin boy, sir?"

"You offerin' to ship out, lad?"

"Yes, sir. I mean, aye, sir."

"Come aboard and let me look at ya." When the boy was on the quarter-deck in front of the captain his head was about level with the big brass buckle on the man's belt. "What's your name?" Childs demanded.

"Matthew Henson, sir. Matthew Alexander Henson."

"And how old be ya, Matthew?"

"Twelve, sir."

Captain Childs said, "You look pretty dirty and raggedy, Matthew. A sailor has to keep himself neat and clean."

"I just walked from Washington, sir."

"All the way from Washington?" The captain was impressed. "Just so you could go to sea?"

"Yes, sir. Do you need a cabin boy?"

"Now, tell the truth, lad—" the captain laid a heavy paw on the boy's shoulder—"what would your folks say if you ran off to sea?"

"My mom and pop are dead."

"Oh? Did you run away from school?"

"No, sir. My Aunt Jenny was gonna send me, but I'd rather go to sea. And she ain't really my aunt. I washed dishes in her restaurant and slept in the kitchen at night. When I told her what I wanted to do, she said it was all right and she give me a dollar."

The captain turned abruptly to a man standing nearby and trumpeted, "Mr. Tracy, this is my new cabin boy, Matthew Alexander Henson. Take him to the fo'c'sle and clean him up and find him a bunk. He's been running afoul some heavy weather and needs rest."

In the following few years Matthew received from Captain Childs a rudimentary education. Of course, he brought to his teacher some special wisdoms, things Childs could never know. He had been born to impoverished sharecroppers in Charles County, Maryland, and he knew the sounds of the night riders of the Ku Klux Klan. Hidden in bushes, he had witnessed the sadism, the obscenities committed by these white men. He knew the worst of life; he was yet to find its compensations. Still, he was surprisingly unscarred. At twelve years of age he was neither aggressive nor submissive; he wanted adventure and he was willing to work for it; there was a simplicity about him, a sturdiness of purpose, and an even disposition. These qualities endeared him to Captain Childs.

They sailed together for six years, south around the Straits of Magellan and across the Pacific to the China Seas, eastward across the Atlantic and into the Baltic. Matt grew up during this time and learned first to read and write, then the skills of an Able-Bodied Seaman. He learned to play the sailor's instrument, the concertina, and developed a true voice. Despite the fact that he was the captain's favorite, he was popular with the crew and was content to remain aboard the *Katie Hines* as long as she sailed.

Matthew was eighteen when Captain Childs died. In grief he quit the *Katie Hines* and shipped aboard a Newfoundland fishing boat. There he learned what it meant to be a Negro in a hostile white crew. There was no wise and protective captain to stand between him and the realities of race prejudice, and he quit the ship for a series of jobs ashore. He was stevedore, chauffeur, messenger, common laborer, and finally stock clerk in the hat store. And now he was back aboard a ship again, bound for Nicaragua with Lieutenant Peary.

Peary was a civil engineer on leave from the Navy to head up this job for the Maritime Canal Company. He was in charge of forty-five engineers and instructed to bring back a survey for a practical canal linking the Pacific and Atlantic Oceans. This was the second expedition the Maritime Canal Company had sent south, and Peary, who had also been on the first one, so impressed his employers that this time he was the engineer in charge.

True, the French were digging a canal in Panama but with little efficiency and not much promise of completion. And everyone knew that the Panama topography was not nearly so good as that which Peary was to survey farther north. In the entire mountain backbone that stretches from Bering Strait in the north to that of Magellan in the south, the lowest pass was along the proposed Nicaragua route. Also, in the center of the isthmus there was large Lake Nicaragua which could accommodate ocean-going vessels, thus reducing the mileage to be dug and locked. A commission of U.S. Army Engineers had previously examined all possible routes in Central America and had recommended this one.

After leaving the United States the ship made one stop at Jamaica to pick up a hundred Negro laborers, then proceeded to the port of San Juan del Norte in Nicaragua and the work began. Peary divided his forces into six land parties, each commanded by a sectional engineer, one hydrographic party, and two boring parties. Peary himself, with Henson, ranged back and forth along the entire 170-mile line between the two oceans, and under the most primitive conditions the two men grew to know each other.

Plunging into the tropical jungle, Peary and Henson found it impossible to advance so much as ten feet without hacking open a path with machetes. They waded through slush and mud waist-deep; they fought insects and the enervating heat. They lay down at night on the banks of turgid rivers with palm leaves for mattresses and the ugly snouts and protuberant eyes of alligators ringing the water's edge to watch over their fitful sleep. The night had no silence; it rang with the screams of tigers, the grunts and splashing of alligators, the howling of monkeys, the whistles and cries of nocturnal birds. Occasionally there came a great booming, like the distant report of a cannon, and its sound echoed through the swamp, bringing fresh cries of alarm from the animals. It was the sound of no army, but the death note of a giant tree in the inland forest as it crashed to earth, carrying with it everything within reach.

Gaining the forest gave Peary and Henson blessed respite from the swamps but it brought its own problems. The trees were true giants: almendro, havilan, gauchipilin, cedar, and cottonwoods rose 200 feet into the air, their great trunks bare until they reached the very tops where a thick tangle of branches and leaves wove a canopy that blotted out the sky and sun. In the permanent twilight below was a tropical thicket made almost impenetrable by vines as thick as a man's arm and stout as the toughest hemp. They bound the underbrush together in an elastic sort of mat that had to be hacked and sawed through before a man could step forward. Even then, the vines crept along the ground to catch the intruders' feet in a mesh from which release could be won only by the use of the machete. The vines caught hold of every projection on a man's clothing, jerking revolvers from belts, wrenching rifles from hands, tearing at buttons, even hanging in loops to catch a man around the throat. After a few days in this nightmare even the swamps seemed beckoning.

Peary ranged through this inhospitable land at a killing pace, but Henson was always at his side, tireless and cheerful. He was personally clean, and his work was neat and methodical, prime requisites in the field. Moreover, he could learn. He became an excellent rifle shot and an expert canoe handler. He was promoted to Peary's personal chain man.

A surveyor's chain is sixty-six feet long and contains one hundred links. The device is used to help the surveyor set distances and triangulate courses. Together Peary and Henson fought through swamp and jungle to run 500 miles of lines and 400 miles of soundings.

Two men living together for seven months under such conditions would normally reveal much of themselves to each other. But not in this case. Peary was efficient, demanding, and withdrawn from his servant. He was scrupulously just in all his dealings, but not intimate. It was only by accident that Henson got a glimpse of the man behind the stern exterior.

They had had a hard day's march and made camp near sundown. Matt had erected the tent, draped the mosquito netting over the opening, made a fire, and was squatted beside it to tend a skillet. Peary was seated on a fallen log, writing in his journal as he did each evening at this time.

Suddenly Peary's hand went to his throat and he gasped out, "My God!"

Henson jumped up and ran to him. "What is it, sir?"

Peary stared at his servant for a moment, his hand still at his throat, his face stricken. When he spoke, however, he had control of himself. "Matt, I've lost the locket."

He referred to a small gold locket Henson had seen suspended around his neck on a slender gold chain. He had never before made any reference to it, but now he spoke as if all men would know the tragedy of its loss.

"When did you last see it, Matt?" he said heavily.

"This morning, I think, Lieutenant. I think you had it when we broke camp."

Peary grimaced. "Search this campsite first, and if we don't find it, we'll have to backtrail."

It was not found in the camp and the two of them started back along the trail, Henson striding out in front.

"Matt!" Peary called sharply. "We must search *every inch* of the trail."

Thereafter they went forward with painful slowness, bent double, their fingers probing the trail as they went. They had covered less than 200 yards when the sun went down and they were forced to return to camp.

After they had eaten, Peary said, "We'll break camp at dawn and backtrail again."

Henson was surprised. He had assumed that their failure to find the locket that evening meant the end of the incident. "How long do we backtrail, sir?"

Peary looked at him and said levelly, "Until we find the locket."

That night Henson had a dream in which he was condemned to a lifetime on his hands and knees, crawling through the jungle in search of a small gold disk that forever eluded him. When he awoke at dawn, the dream became reality. Immediately after breakfast they again backtrailed, both of them bent double, panting with the heat and the strain of the position, their eyes aching and deceiving them, for every bit of moss and pool of water and twisted vine or leaf seemed to glitter gold. They rested briefly at noon, ate some hardtack from their knapsacks, then continued the search.

About an hour later Henson found the locket. It lay in a heel mark, planted deep in decaying vegetation. With a muttered exclamation, Peary snatched it from Henson's hand and examined it minutely. One of the gold links in the chain had given way, and he tinkered with it a moment, forcing the opening closed with two blunt thumbnails. Then, almost reverently, he put the chain around his neck, tucked the locket beneath his shirt, squared his shoulders, and said briskly, "We'll have to double our march, Matt. There's half a day to make up."

"Yes, sir," Henson said. Then he couldn't resist asking, "That locket must be valuable, I guess?"

"Valuable? It's beyond value, Henson. It was given to me by the woman I'm going to marry."

Henson was amazed that his employer could have such a tender emotion. The truth was, Peary was a caldron of emotion. He was an artist of no inconsiderable ability, and he wrote with a vivid, if florid style. When he graduated from Bowdoin College in 1877 he wrote the class ode, the opening stanza of which read:

> Listen, Old Oak,
> Aid I invoke,
> Aid from thy sylvan heart.
> Hush thy soft sighs,
> Bend from the skies,
> Teach me one song ere we part.
> Teach me those mystical, murmurous strains,
> Born of the sunshine, the wind and the rains,
> Give me thy restless wild essence of life,
> Let my verse thrill like an army's wild strife.

The youthful hyperbole was largely under control by the time he met Henson, except where his family was concerned—then he slipped into naked sentimentality.

The emotions that constantly flayed Peary, the symbols with which he ornamented his life, were beyond Henson's comprehension. Even the personal qualities of honor and dignity, which Peary embraced with such uncompromising rigidness, came to the Negro quietly and easily and largely unsought. He was a much less complicated man, to be sure, and he didn't have constantly to square his ambition with his ethics.

If he failed to understand fully the reasons for his employer's postures, he intuitively understood the very human frailties that created them, and he felt a fondness and a protectiveness toward the man.

Peary's field work was completed early in the summer of 1888, and he returned to Washington that July. During the voyage back, Henson speculated on his own future, but not with any real concern. He had seven months' unspent pay in his pocket, enough to sustain himself while he looked around. He would have liked to stay with Peary but the lieutenant was returning to a Navy desk job and there was obviously no need for a partially educated Negro boy there. No matter, something would turn up.

It did. On the last day out from port, Peary summoned him into his cabin and said, "Matt, you did a good job in Nicaragua."

"Thank you, sir," he said. The praise was welcome because it was the first he'd received.

Peary was stretched out in his bunk, arms beneath his head, and for several long moments he studied the bulkhead opposite. When he finally spoke again it was to himself as much as to Henson. "Isn't it amazing that we are almost into the twentieth century and yet there remain thousands upon thousands of square miles on this planet that man has never seen! The Polar caps may be deserts, utterly lifeless places; or they may hide a new breed of man, strange animals and plants. . . . We don't know. For three hundred years the great powers of the world have been sending expeditions north without doing more than touching the edge of the Polar vastness. No man has come within six hundred miles of the North Pole. That land must be explored and claimed by an American. I'm going to do it. Somehow, I'll do it."

Peary removed his eyes from the bulkhead and looked at Henson. "Matt, I'm going to try and organize an expedition to explore North Greenland. Do you want to go along?"

"Well, sir . . ."

"Before you answer, let's face the fact that you are a son of the equator. You were fine in Nicaragua but the North may be hard for you. It will be difficult for all of us, but perhaps especially for you."

If Peary had meant it as a challenge, he achieved his purpose. Henson said, "I'll go north with you, sir, and I think I'll stand it as well as any man."

"I haven't any money, Matt, and I'll have to get some wealthy men to finance the expedition. I may not be able to pay you anything but subsistence and transportation."

"I'll go," Henson said firmly. The implication that a Negro would not survive the North had hardened within him a determination to prove otherwise. Secretly, he wondered if perhaps it was true.

[II]

Upon his return home Peary was put back on active duty at the League Island Navy Yard in Philadelphia. And there he found a job for Henson as his messenger. It was rather grandiose for a Navy lieutenant to have a personal messenger, but Peary was a rather grandiose man.

Henson, a Negro civilian employee in the caste-conscious Navy, was at the very bottom of the social scale; so far down, in fact, that no one bothered even to notice him. It was he who stepped aside in a corridor for another to pass, he who held open the doors, opened and closed windows, delivered messages, all the time the invisible man.

He did his work with quiet and cheerful efficiency, meanwhile observing the fortunes of the man to whom he was committed. Immediately upon returning from Nicaragua, Peary married the girl who had given him the locket. She was Josephine Diebitsch, daughter of Professor Herman H. Diebitsch of the Smithsonian Institution. She was a handsome and aristocratic young lady, a belle of Washington's highest society, yet the all-but-penniless Peary had not been intimidated, and his dash and ardor had carried the day.

Some time after the marriage Peary said to Henson, "I told

Mrs. Peary how you found the locket, Matt. She was pleased."

If there was a touch of *noblesse oblige* in the statement, Matt didn't notice it. He grinned and said, "It was a good thing we found it, sir."

Peary nodded solemnly. "Yes, it was."

Henson also observed the effect upon Peary of the subsequent battle in Washington over the Nicaragua Canal. Peary's plans had been highly praised by his employers and the company was granted a government charter with a capitalization of $100,000,-000. Before the actual digging could begin, however, a treaty between Nicaragua and the United States had to pass the Senate, and before *that* happened it became clear that the French were in deep trouble with their Panama Canal. The French finally offered to sell it to the United States for $40,000,000, and since it was already partly dug, it seemed like a bargain. Congress abandoned the Nicaragua project and authorized President Theodore Roosevelt to buy out the French and complete the Panama Canal. He promptly did so.

Though Peary, along with many other experts, maintained that the Nicaragua route was the preferable one, the defeat of his plan seemed not to affect him at all. Peary had already turned his face north and his days and nights were filled with dogged appeals for funds and endorsements and with maneuvers to obtain another Navy leave.

During April, 1891, a Philadelphia newspaper carried the following item: "Robert E. Peary, Engineer at the Naval Dockyard, is now engaged in fitting out his expedition to North Greenland. As is well known, it is his intention to try to ascertain the extension of Greenland northwards, by undertaking an excursion on sledges over its snow-covered interior. His companions on the expedition are not yet decided upon."

That last sentence did it! Suddenly Henson found himself the buffer between Peary and a flood of applicants for the expedition: college students and professors, soldiers of fortune, military men, athletes, crackpots. They wrote, they telegraphed, they appeared in person, and one by one Henson led them into Peary's office for interviews.

One young applicant, who was eventually chosen to make the expedition, was a Norwegian ski champion by the name of Eivind Astrup. He had read the newspaper clipping, and though he spoke little English, he was determined to try for a place and went to the Navy Yard to demand an audience. He later wrote of this:

I entered the corridors of the dockyard's office, certain of victory. A young man of African origin, afterwards the illustrious "Matt," showed me into Lieutenant Peary's working room, where I was most heartily received. . . . His whole appearance inspired me with absolute confidence. His tall, lean figure was elastic and sinewy; his features, coarse but determined, were aglow with intrepid resolution. Scarcely had our conversation begun before I found myself obliged to pull the friend textbooks out of my pocket. With feverish quickness I ran over the leaves during the remainder of my visit, hardly ever finding the words I wanted, but managing at last, in rather laconic sentences, to give expression to what was in my mind.

In the course of conversation I noticed that Mr. Peary's black servant now and then disappeared through a side door with strange grimaces, returning soon afterwards with an uncomfortably serious and distorted face. He afterwards admitted that this happened whenever he lost control over his risible muscles as he saw me consult my dictionary.[1]

Astrup was not offended by Matt—no one ever was. It was his lively sense of humor that endeared him to people. And here again master and servant differed; for Peary, except when safely in the bosom of his family, had little humor. Peary had a sense of poetry, of destiny, of compassion, of fitness, of justice, of dignity, but little sense of humor, because he strove for perfection.

William Hazlitt wrote, "Man is the only animal that laughs and weeps; for he is the only animal that is struck by the difference between what things are, and what they ought to be."

Peary was determined to make what things were into what they ought to be; thus he could neither weep nor laugh.

As he interviewed the prospective members of his expedition, he had a yardstick by which he measured each man: he visualized him on the trail with food supplies running low and an Arctic storm descending.

On this subject he wrote,

Taking it for granted that in situations requiring great power of endurance and capabilities for resisting hunger, thirst, exposure and fatigue . . . an intelligent and educated man will hold out longer than an ordinary one, and it is will power that does it, the superiority of mind over matter, in what way does this will power act? . . . It is a direct, conscious, painful exertion of the will saying to the body, "You shall not give up. You must keep on. I will make you." . . . an educated man knows better how to take care of himself, how to husband his resources so that every particle of force or stamina, of life itself, shall tell in the bitter struggle. . . .[2]

By this yardstick of education Peary was to make some grievous mistakes in his selection of men. By using this yardstick he long underestimated Henson's qualities.

Among the men who presented themselves as candidates was a Dr. Frederick A. Cook, a surgeon practicing in New York City, who was most personable and twenty-six years of age. His bedside manner could have built a large and lucrative practice, but he had a thirst for adventure. He was young, strong, educated. He met all of Peary's standards. And there was need of a physician on the expedition. He was signed on. In the years to come Peary was to regret that act more than any other one of his life.

In the winter of 1890–91 the American Geographical Society, the Brooklyn Institute, and the Philadelphia Academy of Sciences agreed to sponsor the expedition. Peary obtained leave from the Navy, and the barkentine *Kite*, a sealer, was chartered. Besides the ship's crew, the expedition consisted of Astrup, Dr. Cook, surgeon and ethnologist, Langdon Gibson, ornithologist and chief hunter, John T. Verhoeff, a rather dour mineralogist and meteorologist who not only went without pay (as did all of them) but contributed $2,000, Henson, Peary, and, rather surprisingly (and dismayingly to the rest of the expedition), Mrs. Peary.

Just before departure, Peary called Henson to him and said,

"Matt, here's a paper I'd like you to sign. It is the same state-ment I'm requiring from all members of the expedition." The paper read:

This agreement made between Robert E. Peary, of the United States Navy, and MATTHEW HENSON of Maryland. WITNESSETH: Whereas there is to be undertaken forthwith an expedition to, and into the interior of, Greenland, the same to be known as and called the North Greenland Expedition, of which Expedition said Robert E. Peary is to be sole Commander;

Now therefore, that said MATTHEW HENSON agrees hereby to under-take with the said Peary and said expedition, for the SUCH purposes and objects as said Peary may decide to be practicable and desirable, whether now fully determined or not; and, further,

First: That he, the said MATTHEW HENSON, will faithfully obey all directions and fully carry out all instructions given by the said Peary.

Second: That he will loyally aid and support the said Peary by all means in his power, to accomplish each and every object and purpose of the expedition aforesaid, in such manner as the said Peary shall deem best and require.

Third: That he will not write, or cause to be written or published or furnish to any person such information that such person may write or cause to be printed or published, any newspaper or magazine article or articles, and pamphlet or printed sheet whatever, containing any discussion or description of theories or plans of Greenland explora-tions, the experiences or results of this expedition, or the work of any member thereof, in any shape or manner, until the expiration of four months after the date of the recognized return of the ex-pedition to the place of departure; and further, that he will not write or cause to be written or published, or furnish to any person such information that such person may write or cause to be written or published, any book, pamphlet or narrative whatever, in any way appertaining to, or descriptive of said expedition, or of any theories or plans of Greenland explorations until one year after the complete, regular, official narrative of said expedition, approved by said Peary, shall have been published and offered for sale.

Fourth: That the said Peary, in his capacity of Commander of the Expedition, is to be the sole judge of the time to be devoted to it, the distances to be traversed, the courses to be pursued, the methods and means necessary for the accomplishment of the purposes of the expedition, and the special duties and departments of work for each member thereof, unless he shall authorize some member of the expedition to act for him in one or more of the particulars aforesaid, in which case the said MATTHEW HENSON agrees to yield due obedience to the person designated by said Peary so to act.

Fifth: That all scientific collections made, and all materials acquired by MATTHEW HENSON during the absence of the expedition shall be turned over to said Peary or packed and taken in charge of as said Peary may direct, to become the property of the Academy of Natural Sciences of Philadelphia, Penn.

Sixth: The authority of said Peary to act as herein stipulated shall begin at the time of the departure from the city of New York and continue until the return to the said place of departure.

And the said Peary, in consideration of the above services fairly and justly rendered, and of the other stipulations of said MATTHEW HENSON herein contained, agrees to provide said MATTHEW HENSON with:

First: Subsistence and transportation, befitting such an expedition, during the time intervening between the departure from and return to New York City, of said expedition.

Second: Various items of outfit, viz.: rifle and ammunition, hunting knife and belt, oilskin suit, rubber blanket, sleeping bag, snowshoes, and such other minor items of outfit as said Peary may deem suitable and necessary, or desirable.

Third: To pay him when said expedition shall have returned to New York, the sum of fifty dollars.

The said MATTHEW HENSON hereby pledges his word of honor, as a gentleman, that each item and particular of his agreement herein contained, shall be by him faithfully and unqualifiedly observed.

In witness whereof the said Robert E. Peary and MATTHEW HENSON have to this agreement, executed in triplicate, at PHILADELPHIA hereunto set their hands and affix their seals to this THIRTIETH day of May A.D. 1891.[3]

Henson signed. So did the rest of the expedition, including Dr. Frederick Cook. Thus were planted seeds of contention that were to germinate slowly through many Arctic winters, and come to a bitter and violent fruit eighteen years later.

June 6, 1891, the *Kite* cast off from the pier at the foot of Baltic Street in Brooklyn. She was a small barkentine, a ship having three masts, fore, main, and mizzen. The foremast was square-rigged and the main and mizzen fore and aft rigged. Coal-fired boilers gave her power for a single screw which now churned the harbor waters to carry her up the East River while other craft whistled their salutes and good wishes.

[III]

During the voyage north Peary held staff meetings in his cabin. Though not a member of the staff in a full sense, Henson attended. He was entered on the ship's papers as "personal servant," but there was little valet work on this trip and gradually he became the indispensable handyman, the carpenter and tinker and caulker and cook. But in the meantime he stood quietly in the corner of Peary's cabin and listened and learned while other men made the plans.

Peary tacked a map of Greenland on the bulkhead and it showed the lower half of the land extending into the Atlantic Ocean, the upper half fading into blankness, into the unknown. It was Peary's determination to fill in the northern blankness on that map. He alone of the expedition had some idea of what lay ahead, for he had at least been to the coast of that bleak and mysterious land. In 1886, before going to Nicaragua with Henson, he had made a brief trip to Greenland, buying his own passage on a whaler that dropped him at Godhaven, on Disco Island, the capital of the Danish provincial government.

There he had scraped together what equipment he could, and with a young Danish official sailed across the channel to Greenland's glacial coast. Dragging their sledges behind them, they climbed the glacier and made a brief excursion into the interior, reaching an elevation of 7,500 feet. A blizzard sent them staggering and exhausted back to Disco Island, but Peary was in a state of strange elation. He knew beyond doubt that his destiny was in the North.

As the *Kite* sailed northward past Newfoundland, past Labrador, and prepared to cut into the open Atlantic north-northeast toward Greenland, Peary lectured his party, preparing them for the job ahead. Pointing to the map, he said, "The coast is bold and mountainous, cut by deep fjords and protected by outlying rocky islands. All there is of land, as we know the term, is a ribbon five to twenty-five miles wide along the coast, and it is made up of mountains and valleys and deep fjords. The interior of the country is buried beneath a great white ice cap. We can only guess how it came about. There was probably an accumulation of snow that filled the valleys of the interior until it leveled them even with the mountain summits, and then through the centuries has buried the highest of the mountain summits hundreds and even thousands of feet deep. Now the interior of Greenland is simply an elevated, unbroken plateau of frozen snow eight to ten thousand feet high, a huge, white, glistening shield resting on the mountain tops.

"It is an Arctic Sahara, in comparison with which the African Sahara is insignificant. For on this frozen Sahara occurs no form of life, animal or vegetable; no fragment of rock, no grain of sand. When we get upon it we shall see, except for ourselves, nothing but the infinite expanse of frozen plain, the infinite dome of the cold blue sky, and the cold white sun. Nothing but these."

The cabin was quiet, tense, expectant. When Peary spoke again there was in his words a forced calm that revealed more than anything else could the excitement beneath them. "This plateau, this shield, runs northward we know not how far. It may go all the way to the Pole. It may become the 'imperial highway to the Pole.'"

There followed general discussion, each man concerned with his specialty. Verhoeff, the mineralogist, was hopeful of finding rock specimens along the coast. Gibson demanded from Peary information about bird life. Astrup led a discussion about the comparative merits of snowshoes and skis. Dr. Cook, who had been thoughtful, suddenly said, "Lieutenant, we set up our head-quarters north of Melville Bay?"

"Yes, if the ice conditions will let the *Kite* through that far."

"No habitation there, I suppose?"

"No," said Peary. "The Danes live south of 73 degrees north latitude. I hope to make 76 or 77 degrees."

"What about the aborigines, the Eskimos?"

"Yes, there is a tribe there, the most northerly people of the earth."

"I have my camera with me," Cook said. "If we could make contact with them, and then photograph and measure them, we could bring back some valuable ethnological information."

"Quite so," Peary agreed.

Two people did not enter into the conversation. First, there was Mrs. Peary, the newlywed who saw no reason to be separated from her husband just because he was headed into an unexplored wilderness. She sat quietly and serenely in her silk brocade dress, adding a touch of elegance to the sealer's dark and pitching cabin. She busied herself with needlework. Matthew Henson merely leaned against the bulkhead. He, as yet, had no specialty.

Only a modest amount of equipment was aboard ship, partly because the expedition had limited funds, but also out of igno-rance. No one knew what they would face in the North. They had tea, coffee, sugar, and milk sufficient to last two years, but little meat because they expected to live off game in the area. There were two sledges and timber to make additional ones, snowshoes, skis, moccasins, rubber ice creepers, and an abundance of woolen clothing, much of which was to be found entirely unsuited to Arctic work. There was a variety of firearms and ammunition, along with navigational, meteorological, and photo-graphic equipment. On the forward deck was lashed the lumber for a twelve-by-twenty-foot house which was to be constructed on the beach and serve as living space and headquarters when the ship returned south for the winter. Six men and a woman were to live in that small space through the unknown terrors of the six-month-long Arctic night.

On June 11, the fifth day out of New York, the *Kite* steamed into Sydney Harbor, Nova Scotia, to take aboard coal. When her waist and part of her quarter-deck were piled high with coal, she headed north into the Strait of Belle Isle and her first Arctic storm. She pitched and dipped and rolled as tons of water poured over her and ice began to attack her flanks. The ice thickened into a pack and she had to search for leads of open water to take her farther north.

The ice pack rose and fell with the undulations of the sea, and it roared with a sound ten times that of any surf. The ship creaked and moaned with its own pain, and the members of the expedition were violently seasick. Yet the storm was not severe by Arctic standards; it was the merest flick of nature's whip.

Throughout it all Henson, who was a seaman after all, moved about the ship with sure step and cheerfully ministered to those who, with green faces, clung to their bunks.

The poorest sailors came out of their bunks, however, when Greenland was sighted on the morning of June 23. Cape Desolation rose out of the sea on the starboard bow and everyone crowded to the rails. Soon there was a full view of the coast, the inland peak of Kangarsuck, 4,710 feet high, rearing its snow-blotched apex to look like a Matterhorn; and next to it the great marble wall of the Frederikshaab Glacier, one of the largest in the world.

They moved northward along the coast, making their way through the floes with slow and careful maneuvers. Terns and auks wheeled overhead to shrill at the invaders, and sleek seals looked up from the floes to stare with surprise and then slide silently into the black waters. Then Henson saw his first iceberg!

Greenland produced these wonders of nature. The mass of glacial ice moved down the coastal valleys under the pressure of gravity, extended into the water until the ice broke off and floated out to sea. About one-ninth of the mass appeared above water, but what a sight was that small fragment of the total!

Out of a hundred fathoms of water the berg towered high above the *Kite*, and it had been shaped by the wind and sun into fantastically beautiful cliffs and grottoes. At its base great arches had been carved out by the pounding sea and within them rainbows streaked the ice with color. The lofty peaks were being eroded by the sun, and waterfalls cascaded down and down and finally spilled into the sea.

Henson had been joined at the rail of the *Kite* by Peary and the rest of the members of the expedition and all the crew who could safely leave their duties. While they stared in silent wonder, they heard a sudden rumble, like the sound of distant drums. The rumble grew louder, became a cannonading, a full battle, angrier and angrier, culminating in a series of shattering explosions. Before their eyes the iceberg began to break up. A part of the giant majestically heeled over and slid into the sea.

There was an enraged hissing and boiling of the water, then an enormous wave rose up and began to race toward the *Kite*. The ice pack stood protectively between the wave and the ship, but even it could not resist the force of the savage water. As tremendous pressure was exerted from beneath, the ice pack broke open with a series of thunderclaps. Large pieces of ice were thrown in all directions, skidding along the pack surface with deafening screams.

There was a chaos of sound and sight that stunned the senses, and those aboard the frail bit of wood and iron could only cling to the railing and pray.

The wave had largely spent itself by the time it reached the ship, but even so the *Kite* rolled violently as the ice broke about her and bit savagely at her hull. Men were thrown about the deck, staggered to their feet to be thrown again. Fortunately, no one went overboard; no one was badly injured. The ship and crew survived but with a bleak sort of awareness that they were many miles from their goal.

On Saturday, June 27, the *Kite* put in at Godhaven, the chief settlement of the North Inspectorate of Danish Greenland. Lieutenant and Mrs. Peary were received and entertained by the Inspector and his wife. All the expedition, with the exception of Henson, dined with the local officials. After a few days of such amenities, the *Kite* steamed on north and engaged in the long struggle with the ice pack in Melville Bay.

The plan was for the *Kite* to batter her way through the summer ice as far as Inglefield Gulf, 77 degrees north latitude, and there put the expedition ashore where they would spend the long Arctic winter, letting the ship and her crew retreat south to safety. They were almost within sight of their destination when an accident occurred that threatened to put an end to the entire project.

At eight o'clock on Saturday evening, July 11, Henson was leaning on the forward railing, watching the *Kite*'s labors. She was ramming a passageway through relatively heavy ice, her sharp bow forcing a crack, then backing off to come forward again at full speed to widen the crack. The ship bucked and rolled, her riggings lashed, dishes and all things loose slid and clattered.

Peary suddenly appeared and stood beside Henson. The two of them braced themselves against the ship's thrusts for several minutes. Then Matt said, "Not like Nicaragua, is it, sir?"

"Not much." Peary smiled. Then he looked rather searchingly at the Negro and said, "How are you making out, Matt?"

Immediately Henson knew what was on his mind. Peary had always euphemistically called him a "son of the tropics," and was doubtful that such a man could function well in the North. No slight was intended by the question; it was honest concern.

"I can see how the North gets into a man," Matt said carefully. "It's got into me. I feel like I never want to leave it."

For some moments Peary thought on the answer, words that said much or little, then turned and went aft to observe the ship from the stern. Henson didn't turn to watch his going; he kept his eyes on the ice ahead.

The ship made several more lunges, then as she backed off

there was a muffled, bumping sound, and her stern swung sharply to port. The sound and the movement seemed of no particular importance, and for a time Henson continued looking ahead, waiting for the ship to return to the attack. When she didn't, he looked aft casually and saw the helmsman running toward a man who writhed on deck. The man in agony was Peary.

The bump that had gone through the ship was a large cake of ice striking the rudder, jamming it hard over and tearing the wheel from the hands of the two men on duty. One of them had been thrown clear across the deck. The long, heavy iron tiller had swept over the afterdeck where Peary was standing and, acting like a scythe, brought him down. Both bones of his right leg were snapped above the ankle.

Henson knelt beside his lieutenant to cushion his head. Through clenched teeth Peary ordered, "Get Doctor Cook." When Cook arrived, he deftly examined the leg and then ordered the men to carry Peary to his cabin. Henson, the two helmsmen, and Gibson carried the wounded man across the littered deck and down the companionway. In his agony Peary uttered not a sound.

Peary's leg was set and strapped into a narrow wooden box Henson built for the purpose. Henson's duties were now expanded to that of nursemaid, and along with Mrs. Peary he tended the lieutenant through the feverish, pain-racked days and nights that immediately followed.

Everyone on the expedition agreed that they would now have to turn around and go home. Everyone but Peary. When the idea was first broached to him, he angrily brushed it aside. Finally Cook stepped forward with his opinion as a doctor.

"It's going to be difficult enough for a man to survive the winter up here in good health," Cook said, "but with a broken leg . . ."

Peary interrupted him, demanding briskly, "How long before I can walk on this leg, Doctor?"

Cook shrugged. "Four or five months, perhaps. Depends."

After rapid calculation, Peary said, "That will be into next year. I'll be ready, then, to make the spring march onto the ice cap."

"Perhaps so, *if* you survive."

"I'll survive, Doctor."

"But when we arrive at Inglefield Gulf, you won't even be able to get ashore."

"I'll have my men strap me on a board and carry me ashore."

"And then what?" Cook demanded.

"Before too many weeks I'll have Henson make me some crutches."

"You plan to travel on crutches . . . on the *ice?*" Cook was incredulous.

"On the ice," Peary said firmly. "I'm sorry to ignore your advice, Doctor, but people invested a lot of money in this expedition and my first responsibility is to them. For no reason of *my own health* will I turn back."

When the *Kite* arrived at Inglefield Gulf in late July, they found it choked with an impenetrable ice pack, but just north of it was McCormick Bay, a small inlet at the foot of a towering, red, lichen-covered cliff. At the head of the bay was a glacier which seemed to promise access to the ice cap above. Peary, reclining on deck and with his leg packed in the wooden box, studied the shore and determined that the winter headquarters should be here.

The *Kite* was driven against the ice foot that extended from land about fifty yards, and upon this supplies were unloaded and dragged ashore. Strapped to a large plank and carried by Henson and three sailors, Peary was first over the side. Then went the food and weapons and expedition equipment, and finally the lumber for the house that would shelter them. It had been precut and had only to be erected and nailed together, but that was an enormous job for one man. And generally it was one man who did it—Henson.

Cook, Gibson, Astrup, and Verhoeff were, after all, unpaid volunteers, and while they submitted to discipline (often grudgingly), Henson was the servant and he submitted automatically.

The interior dimensions of the building were twenty-one feet by twelve feet. A good third of this had to be partitioned off as private quarters for the lieutenant and his wife. The outside was an airtight shell composed of sheathing and closely fitted boards and two thicknesses of tarred paper. The inner shell was composed of thick trunk boards and heavy brown paper. And inside this, Indian blankets covered the walls and floor. It gave the place a sort of oriental atmosphere.

Around the outside of the entire house, about three feet away, was built a five-foot-high wall of supply boxes. This was roofed over with canvas. Thus, when the winter snows came and covered everything, it would be possible to step out of the house and into a tunnel lined with supply boxes full of food and fuel. When the structure was completed it was named Red Cliff House.

At 5:30 A.M. on July 30 the *Kite* gave a whistle and her crew stood along the railing to wave good-by to the small band that stood on shore. Now, for good or ill, six men and a woman were committed to the coming Arctic night.

While Peary fretted at his infirmity, the rest of the expedition were excitedly exploring the countryside, bringing back new specimens of flowers and rocks, hunting reindeer, foxes, and the white Arctic hare. And shortly after the second week had begun Gibson and Verhoeff came back with a load of decaying, gelatinous substance that could be smelled a hundred yards off. Everyone gathered around excitedly, for this was whale meat and blubber. It had been found in a cache nearby, and this meant there were Eskimos some place in the area. Remembering Peary's promise to let him take ethnological measurements and pictures, Dr. Cook was particularly excited and asked that he be permitted to go on an expedition to find the Eskimos. Peary could have said only the word "yes," but his habit was military and he put his orders in writing:

Dr. F. A. Cook, Surgeon and Ethnologist. Sir: You will be second in command of the boat expedition to Herbert, Northumberland, and Haklayt Islands, and, in event of serious accident to Mr. Gibson, will assume the command. During the absence of the expedition you will note carefully the location of all Eskimo houses and villages on the shores visited, and will take full descriptive notes of them, mode of construction, size, material, etc. Should you find natives, you will endeavor to obtain from them reindeer, and bear, and blue fox skins, and especially kamiks.* You will endeavor to make the natives understand the location of the house and the fact that they can find there desirable articles in exchange for their furs and implements. If practicable, induce a man and woman, possessors of a kayak and accessories, to return with you and settle for the winter near the house. If you do not succeed in this you may be able to bring a man with his kayak back with you. As an inducement you can perhaps convey to him the idea of his having a gun to use. R. E. Peary, U.S.N. Commanding Expedition.[4]

The expedition, with Gibson, Astrup, Cook, and Verhoeff, took the whaleboat *Faith* (previously removed from the *Kite*) and were off to the islands on August 12, leaving Henson to complete Red Cliff House, Mrs. Peary to arrange its furnishing, and Peary to shoot game from a sitting position on the shore. Six days later the tiny sail on the whaleboat hove into view and Peary, assisted by Henson, hobbled to welcome it, and to his great delight found an Eskimo family aboard. They had come, with their worldly belongings, to camp outside Red Cliff House through the winter.

They jumped ashore eagerly and made directly for Mrs. Peary. They had never seen a white woman and they slowly circled her. They were short, hardly coming to Mrs. Peary's shoulder, and they looked up with gathering amusement in their black eyes. They began to giggle. They pointed to the carefully braided hair piled high on Mrs. Peary's head, and to the fashionable hat that surmounted that; they pointed to the leg-of-mutton sleeves, to the closely fitted bodice in front and the bustle that projected behind; and suddenly it was just all too funny and they roared with laughter. They rolled on the ground and slapped their sides and gasped for breath.

Slowly they recovered, took a fresh look, and went into another seizure. They found this tall, stately woman, the personifica-

* Eskimo fur boots.

tion of nineteenth-century civilization and culture, ludicrous beyond anything they had seen. Mrs. Peary endured it all with composure, her husband with stiff dignity. Peary knew that the two rolling and howling Eskimos did not mean to be offensive, but he was slightly offended just the same.

When Ikwah and his wife had finally laughed themselves out, they saw Henson standing a bit apart and now made for him, circled him, and talked to each other excitedly. They did not laugh this time, but they smiled and made gestures that no one could interpret. Finally, Ikwah grabbed Henson by the arm, pulled up his sleeve, and held Henson's arm next to his own. The skin colors were almost the same.

"Innuit . . . Innuit!" Ikwah said again and again with a big grin on his face.

Ikwah was from the Smith Sound tribe, but all Eskimos called themselves Innuit, which meant inner self, the spirit, the soul. He had mistaken Henson for another Eskimo. It was all logical, to his simple mind. The only men he had ever seen outside his tribe were "kabloonas," the white men who had brought him here in the whaleboat. He reasoned that the world must be populated by Eskimos and white men. Henson was obviously not a white man; therefore he must be an Eskimo. He must be a brother.

When Henson finally understood what Ikwah was trying to say, he laughed and threw his arms around the little Eskimo. With that embrace there began the legend about Miy Paluk, the name the Eskimos gave the man who was a Negro in all eyes but theirs.

[IV]

News of the encampment of white men soon reached back to the rest of the Smith Sound tribe of Eskimos and other families began to arrive. Peary put the Eskimo women to work making fur garments for the expedition, and he sent the Eskimo men on hunting expeditions; and throughout it all Eskimo and white men studied each other with mutual amazement.

Dr. Cook undertook his ethnological studies, and as each new Eskimo arrived, he or she was taken into warm Red Cliff House and urged to remove all clothing so that Cook could take photographs and record bodily measurements. There was no false modesty among the Eskimos, in fact, no modesty at all, but it did seem to them a strange procedure. They submitted with good humor, as they did to all of the white men's crazinesses.

These Innuit Eskimos had strikingly Mongolian features, and the theory of their presence in this northland is based upon this oriental characteristic. These people are believed to be the remnants of an ancient Siberian tribe that was driven from their home out onto the Arctic Ocean by the fierce Tartar invasion in the Middle Ages. They gradually moved eastward to drift down the Northern Greenland Archipelago and settle along the shores of Smith Sound. The tribe was found to number 253. They were the most northerly race in the world, living in complete isolation and independence in a most savage environment. They could have stepped right out of the Stone Age.

They had no government, no religion, no money or standard of value, no written language, no property except their dogs and weapons; their food was nothing but meat, blood, and blubber, and their clothing was the skins of birds and animals. Their constant occupation in life was to capture enough birds and animals to feed and clothe themselves.

And there were a few more things they lacked: they had no jealousies, no intoxicants, no infectious diseases, no murders, no cops or courts, no soldiers, no wars. These shortcomings would place them at the bottom of the scale of civilization, but they were completely indifferent to this because they had no conception of the outside world. They were a simple, happy people who were quick, intelligent, ingenious, and thoroughly human.

One more thing must be said about them: they had no deodorants—no roll-on, no spray-on, no rub-on—and they smelled. Their first impact on the Peary expedition was that of the persistent, everlasting smell. The source was their diet of seal and pure essence of blubber. This bouquet was spiced up a bit by an admixture of walrus, narwhal, and polar bear. With the exception of Mrs. Peary, the expedition soon became accustomed to the smell, grew even not to notice it.

Peary paid for the Eskimo services with food, knives, needles and thread, guns and ammunition. He established, from the beginning, a reputation for honest dealing and the meticulous keeping of his word. The Eskimos called him Pearyaksoah, which meant Big Peary. This was a compliment, a measure of their respect, and from it one might think that their primary interest was in this man who was so big and so different from them in so many ways. But no, their overwhelming interest was in Henson, a man more like themselves. Ikwah and his friend, Ahnalka, took it upon themselves to teach Henson the Eskimo language, one of the most difficult in the world.

Moravian missionaries have spent thirty and even forty years with Eskimos without fully mastering the language. Latin, Greek, French, and German are comparatively easy beside Eskimo. In the process of writing an Eskimo dictionary for the armed forces during World War II, Admiral Donald MacMillan arranged alphabetically and spelled phonetically 3,037 words and admitted there were more to be added.

Each Eskimo word is exact, decisive, fully expressive. Where the English language might require an entire sentence to explain something, the Eskimos do it with a single word. Henson, the least educated of all the men on the expedition, became the most proficient in this difficult language. But then, he got more tutoring than anyone else. His new friends were deliriously happy each time he mastered a new phrase, and they always prepared a suitable celebration.

One afternoon Ikwah came up to him and demanded, "*Karket?*" (Are you hungry?)

Henson thought a moment and answered, "*Kark-punga.*" (I am hungry.)

"*Nerri-katti-giniar-pittigut?*" demanded Ikwah. (Will you eat with us?)

Henson replied, "*Nerri-katti-giniar pagit.*" (I will eat with you.)

Ikwah laughed and clapped his hands together in pleasure, then grabbed Henson by the arm to lead him to the family igloo. This had not been just a language lesson but a formal invitation to dinner.

The Eskimos, when first arriving at Red Cliff House, had lived in their tupiks (skin tents), but now with winter approaching Ikwah and his wife had constructed their stone igloo. It was a structure half excavated beneath and half built above the ground surface and covered an area of twelve by fourteen feet. The walls were built of stone and sod and, using the cantilever principle, massive stones covered over the roof. A stone tunnel gave entrance, and though it was never closed it was so skillfully constructed that no draft or current of air disturbed the quiet interior.

Just inside the entrance was a small area of standing room, and on either side were alcoves for the storage of meat and stone lamps. On the far end was a raised platform made of flat stones and covered with furs, the family bed. A single small window of seal intestines over the entrance admitted a little light.

Henson crawled through the tunnel, and when he stood erect he faced not just Ikwah's family but several others who had come for the occasion. Body heat had driven the temperature upward and everyone was stripped to the waist.

Remembering his manners, Henson cried, "*Sainak sunai! Sainak sunai!*" (Wonderful pleasure and happy to be here.)

The circle of brown faces cried back, "*Assukiak, assukiak!*" (The same with us, you are right.) Then everyone laughed and laughed, for no reason other than good health and love.

This was to be a feast of a very special delicacy—Giviaq, little auk birds pickled in oil. What made it so special was not only the flavor, but the long and painstaking care in its preparation. In the spring a hunter kills a seal and skins it through the mouth without puncturing any of the skin. Not every hunter can do this, and even the most skillful hunter can't do it every time. But when it is accomplished there is created a magnificent poke with the seal blubber clinging to the inside. The hunter takes this poke to the cliffs where the auks nest, catches them in nets, and stuffs them into his poke until it is full up. He ties the opening with a rawhide thong, then buries it under stones. Through the long summer the blubber turns to oil and soaks the birds, which slowly decompose. When winter comes the whole thing freezes and can be kept outside the igloo to be available for special occasions.

When Henson entered the igloo, there lay the partially thawed and distended sealskin. After the greetings had been said, Ikwah chopped open the poke to reveal the birds. Demonstrating the method of eating them for Henson, he removed one and began to pluck the feathers which, over the summer, had turned from white to pink. They pulled out easily, and when the small bird was quite naked, he bit off the legs and chewed them down. Then,

with a deft twist of the wrist, he removed the skin from the
bill backwards, turned it inside out, and sucked off the fat. Then
he ate the skin. Now at last the meat of the bird was eaten. Ikwah
handed a second bird to Henson.

Matt did his best to follow the ritual. He was not as skillful as
his host, but it was a passable performance and the assembly laughed
and clapped their hands. Now everyone dug into the poke. And
when it was finally empty they searched with their fingers among
the remains for the viscera, especially the chunks of frozen blood.
Once able to divorce his mind from the anatomy of the meal,
Henson found it all quite delicious.

"*Nak-ko-mek, nak-ko-mek* (thanks)," he murmured, too full
to be able to speak aloud.

But food was just the beginning of the celebration; now there
was to be music—or what the Eskimos considered music. Their
culture had not advanced far in this direction, as was soon ap-
parent. Their sole instrument was the ayayut, a drum made of
the skin of a walrus throat stretched over a round frame of bone
to which a handle was attached. It was beaten with a piece of
bone to set the tempo in accompaniment of the human voice.

Everyone present knew that Ahnalka was considered a good
singer and would be the man to perform now. Still, there was an
elaborate ritual that had to be followed before he would begin.
He had to appear modest and reluctant and only finally consent
under the great pressure of all present. The dialogue that pre-
ceded the singing was so standard as to be almost a stylized part
of the performance.

Ikwah began it by saying, "Ahnalka, it would give us pleasure
if you would sing tonight."

"No," Ahnalka replied, "I do not feel like singing tonight."

"But you are one of the best singers."

"I am nothing. I do not know how to sing. Besides, I am not
in the mood. No man can be made to sing when he does not
feel like it."

Henson did not follow the dialogue completely but he saw the
firm and final rejection on Ahnalka's part and he thought this

was surely the end. But instead, Ikwah pulled out a drum from under the bed furs, tightened the skin on it by licking it with his tongue, then handed it to Ahnalka.

"Why do you give it to me?" Ahnalka cried. "I do not know how to sing. No one would want to hear me. I am terrible."

Immediately they all shouted their belief in Ahnalka's skill and their determination to hear him sing just one really fine song. "*Qa, qa*," they cried, "come on. We are all so happy to have a really fine singer in our midst."

Ahnalka frowned at the drum in his hands, acting as if everyone had lost his senses. Then, with the greatest reluctance, he agreed to sing. But now he announced that of course he couldn't perform alone, his voice was too poor for that, Ikwah would have to join him.

The same procedure was repeated, this time Ikwah refusing, saying how poor he was, and the rest of them assuring him he was excellent. Finally he, too, agreed to perform. Now followed an interminable argument between the two as to who was to sing and who play the ayayut. At last it was decided that Ahnalka should sing and Ikwah play the drum. The negotiations had consumed a half hour.

Ahnalka now stood up and took his position in the middle of the circle of eager brown faces. All light but a single candle was extinguished. The drum began the rhythm, a triple beat—boom, boom, boom. The seated bodies began to sway. Ahnalka began to sing. An almost tuneless chant slowly developed a charge of emotion. As he sang he swayed to the rhythm, but never moved his feet. He began to make horrible faces and horrible sounds to match; no recognizable words came out of his mouth, just wails and grunts and cries. The circle of spectators, now under his spell, began to join in with their own chant and the drum grew louder. Now the whole audience was possessed by the song, emotions mounting to a frightening pitch.

There was a formalized way of ending the song. To discharge the mass emotions, Ahnalka would be required to clown, to create laughter. He began to bend toward Ikwah, the drummer. Ikwah diminished the beat, finally giving it up entirely. Gripping the bone drumstick, he brandished it before Ahnalka's nose. At this gesture Ahnalka took up a long wail, "Ay, ay, ay, ay, ay, ay!" Ikwah joined him, matching the vowels with all his lung power. The two men screamed until they were exhausted and both fell back in laughter. Relieved, the audience now broke into laughter too, and the song was ended.

Suddenly, to everyone's amazement and delight, Henson announced he would sing. He stood up, and all eyes expected to see him take the traditional place in the middle of the circle and sway and chant to the beat of the drum, but instead he walked over to the storage platform by the entrance tunnel and reached for the duffel bag he had inconspicuously placed there when entering. From the bag he removed his battered concertina and then resumed his place in the circle. Everyone crowded around to look at and touch the strange thing he held. And when he played a series of notes, there was a gasp of astonishment.

Their amazed chattering stilled when Henson began to sing and accompany himself. He sang the only songs he knew, the hymns he had learned as a child aboard the *Katie Hines*. He sang "The Old Rugged Cross," "Rock of Ages," and finally "In the Garden." His baritone voice filled the rock igloo with words and music meaningless to his audience, and yet they responded to the sweetness of the sound. He sang:

> I walk in the garden alone,
> When the dew is sweet on the roses.
> And the voice I hear
> Ringing in my ear,
> The Son of God discloses.
> And . . . I walk with Him
> And I talk with Him,
> And He tells me I am His own.
> And the joys we share
> As we tarry there,
> None other has ever known.

Verhoeff and Gibson, returning from a hunting trip, happened by Ikwah's igloo at this moment. They stood outside the stone tunnel to listen to Henson's voice drift out into the crisp Arctic night, sounds such as this air had never before carried.

Verhoeff said with a wink, "I thought Matt had gone native but I guess I was wrong. He's in there trying to convert the heathen."

He was wrong again. Throughout his life Henson found the Eskimos quite wonderful just the way they were.

[V]

As the Arctic night approached, Peary sent out Astrup, Cook, Gibson, and Verhoeff to practice sledging and skiing and snow-shoeing on the ice cap, and to lay down caches of food supplies to be used during the explorations the following spring. Henson's duties were pretty much confined to the house and camp. He was cook and housekeeper and general handyman, a servant instead of a full member of the expedition.

This was what he had expected, as he had hired himself out, and if he had ambitions to be something more, he did not express them. He was the efficient and smiling "boy," always at Mrs. Peary's elbow when she needed him.

Though Red Cliff House was in savage country, Mrs. Peary was determined to make it an outpost of civilization, determined that the men would not forget their manners. Hers was the attitude of the British Colonial who never surrenders his tea at four and always dresses for dinner at eight. She could not carry things that far, of course, but she did demand that the men be shaved at dinner, that they watch their language, that they generally behave themselves as gentlemen. This was to cause some tensions and resentments as the Arctic night drew on, but she was a strong-willed woman and thought she knew what was best for morale. Certainly she knew what was best for *her* morale. Hardly more than a bride, a woman of culture and position, she was dropped into a place of primitive hardships such as few women of her class had known. She faced up to it in her own way, and whatever else, it was a brave way.

As part of the regimen of civilization and manners, she announced that each man's birthday would be observed with a proper dinner, served with the proper wine. The man to be so honored could choose his own menu from the supplies available and from the game that could be killed. The first birthday that arrived in August was Matt Henson's.

Matt chose the menu and Mrs. Peary cheerfully cooked it. It was: mock-turtle soup, stew of little auk with green peas, broiled breasts of eider duck, Boston baked beans, corn, tomatoes, apricot pie, plum duff, sliced peaches, brandy and coffee.

Matt sat at the head of the table in the place of honor; all toasted him and sang "Happy Birthday." Peary entered in his journal the fact that they had given the party for "my loyal colored boy." The aristocratic Mrs. Peary carried it through with spirit.

After the meal had ended Mrs. Peary proposed that some sweets be given to the "pickaninnies." She meant the Eskimo children living in the igloos surrounding Red Cliff House. She was using the language of the times and certainly Henson was not offended. She was unconsciously accepting the Eskimo point of view—that Henson was their brother.

The Arctic night was from September to February and it was a time of trial for those living in the confined quarters of Red Cliff House. The long months of darkness and storms created stresses that only the most sanguine (or most disciplined) of men could endure without fears for their own sanity. The leader and the servant of this expedition were the two men who found the least terror in the night. Peary was so full of plans and responsibilities for the coming spring that he saw the winter as only a hindrance. Henson was deeply involved with the Eskimos and was sharing their therapy of games and laughter.

The other members of the expedition, Cook, Astrup, Gibson, and Verhoeff, responded variously according to temperament, but all with apprehensions. The fact that Peary and his wife had private quarters within the house was sufficient in Dr. Cook's eyes to create plots and counterplots. In his unpublished journal he even stated suspicions of Henson: "Serving as camp cook and general servant to Peary and his wife, he [Henson] had not much time to go astray. He was impulsive and unwise in his remarks. Coming to the men he would carry tales from the inner quarters, and we figured that he would do the same from our campfires. Henson was believed to be a secret service messenger of the grapevine order and he suffered from this suspicion."[5] And later he wrote, "There was mutiny in the air."

Cook, a man of well-known imagination, overstated the case, but certainly there was tension that winter. And only Henson could escape into the Eskimo igloos and ignore the white men's suspicion of each other.

There was beauty to behold that fall and winter. First came the awesome auroras, ghostly and shimmering veils of colored light that hung in the sky. They are caused by atomic particles ejected by the sun and entering the earth's atmosphere near the magnetic pole. When they collide with particles of nitrogen and oxygen they glow in weird beauty. The colors of the lights depend on the altitude of the collision and the wave length of the particles involved. Collisions 600 miles up create luminous sheets of blue; those from 50 to 175 miles up produce yellow and green coronas. In the lower levels the auroras take on the forms of vast waterfalls and celestial arches and grottoes. The light of the more brilliant ones can be seen as far south as Mexico City, but for our explorers, it was so close as to drape the shoulders and dazzle the eyes.

When fall passed so did the aurora, replaced by the crashing darkness which alternated with frozen moonlight. Henson heard the fettered sea cry beneath its crust of ice. He marched to the feet of the savage black cliffs, the shattered bones of earth's primeval skeleton, all of it caught in devilish splendor.

The Eskimos knew when the moon would appear, never missing by a day. They could tell by the dimming of the stars and the disappearance of those of fifth and sixth magnitude. They considered the stars the spirits of their ancestors. The Big Dipper was, they explained to Henson, seven reindeer feeding on the hills of heaven. The Pleiades, the Seven Sisters, were a team of dogs in pursuit of a bear. The three stars in Orion's Belt were three steps cut in the face of a celestial glacier. To them heaven was not a better place than earth, not a place of justice and reward, but more of what existed here on earth.

Thus, when a man died, his hunting outfit was buried with him, and his dogs strangled so they might join him in future hunts. When a woman died, she was buried with cooking pots. The Eskimos were quite content with life on earth and could think of nothing much better in the hereafter, with one exception—in the hereafter they would be free of the evil spirits that plagued them on earth.

Tornarsuit were the evil spirits of the North, and the greatest of these, the Devil, was Torngak. He was the moaning of the wind and the cry of the sea ice. He would stand outside an igloo for hours, listening, always listening. He must from time to time be driven away with shouts and brandishing of harpoons. He presses most closely upon a man when he is far from home, and when it is dark and cold.

Henson was introduced to the intimacies of family life. He learned that the husband is the ruler, in fact the dictator, of the household. The wife is completely subservient, to the point almost of chattel. She undertakes no tasks her husband does not direct, and refuses none he has determined upon. A husband may, as a gesture of generosity and friendship, offer his wife to a neighbor or visitor for the night. She would not think of objecting to such an arrangement. And if a child results from such generosity, the husband happily undertakes its support. There were not many Eskimo children born, and those who did survive were loved and pampered by all. And besides, the husband may have some children of his own being born and cared for in neighboring igloos. It all worked out pretty even.

The arrival of the Peary expedition resulted, inevitably, in some complications. A week after Ikwah and his family had set up housekeeping outside Red Cliff House, the Eskimo looked Mrs. Peary over with a speculative eye and suggested to Peary that they swap wives for the night. Peary refused and Ikwah went away bewildered and offended. Peary and Henson went to considerable lengths to explain to Ikwah that no offense was intended; it just was the white man's custom *not* to swap wives. The Eskimo was amazed at the strange custom.

A more serious incident occurred during the winter night. The various Eskimo men had, in return for knives and guns, hired out their wives as servants to members of the expedition. The women were hired primarily as seamstresses, making the fur winter garments to be used on the trail. Astrup's servant was the extremely young wife of the Eskimo named Qolugtinguaq.

Astrup, nerves strung tight because of the gloom and the storms of the long night, began to demand excessive service from the young girl, and one afternoon when she didn't come quickly at his call, he crossed the room of Red Cliff House and slapped her in the face. Shock and tears followed, and she ran out of the house and to her husband in her own igloo.

Peary spoke sternly to Astrup about the incident, not only because he objected to the physical violence but also because he feared such happenings would jeopardize their relationship with the Eskimos. For a few days the members of the expedition watched carefully for any signs of resentment by Qolugtinguaq, the husband, but there was none. The incident passed and was apparently forgotten.

Only Henson, of all the expedition, learned that Astrup had put the husband in a cruel dilemma. One evening in Qolugtinguaq's igloo the conversation got around to Astrup, and Henson asked, "How did it happen that you allowed that to pass? You might have at least complained to Pearyaksoah."

Qolugtinguaq said quickly, "You do not understand, Miy Paluk."

"I hoped you could make me understand," Henson said.

"My wife is a child. A man who gets angry with a mere child is not worth bothering with."

Henson recognized the Eskimo logic in this, but he suspected there was something more. Qolugtinguaq frowned at his boots, and finally spoke his real problem. "If I had objected to Astrup striking my wife, I would have revealed how devoted to her I am, how much I depend upon her, and that would have made me ridiculous before all men."

"*Tukki-si-vunga* (I understand)," Henson said softly.

Qolugtinguaq flashed him a grateful smile, now convinced more than ever that Henson must be some sort of Eskimo.

During the long night the members of the expedition knew work as well as quarrels. The most important of all lessons was the mastery and use of the Eskimo dog. Aside from man, the dog was the sole motive power available, and Peary would have to depend upon dogs to get him across the ice cap and back again.

These magnificent animals, descendants of the Arctic wolf, can do more work on less food than any animal in the world. A month-old puppy is hardy enough to stand the coldest weather in the open.

The Eskimo dogs come in a variety of markings and colors: gray, black, yellow, brown, and mottled, but the pure-blooded types have pointed muzzles, sharp-pointed ears, wide-set eyes, a shabby coat and bushy tail, and are marked like their ancestors, the Arctic white wolf.

The Eskimos sold their dogs and sledges to the expedition and gave lessons in their use. To handle these half-wild creatures required skill and strength and courage. Not at all to the Eskimos' surprise, Henson was the most apt pupil they had. He loved the dogs, to begin with, but on top of that he didn't fear them or fear to discipline them. He had a true Eskimo's approach, and he was soon as skilled as any man in the tribe.

Henson wrote of these animals:

The dogs are ever interesting. They never bark, and often bite, but there is no danger from their bites. To get together a team that has not been tied down the night before is a job. You take a piece of meat, frozen as stiff as a piece of iron, in one hand, and the harness in the other, you single out the cur you are after, make proper advances, and when he comes sniffling and snuffling and all the time keeping at a safe distance, you drop the sheet iron on the snow and the brute makes a dive, and you make a flop, you grab the nearest thing grabbable—ear, leg, or bunch of hair—and do your best to catch his throat, after which, everything is easy. Slip the harness over the head, push the forepaws through, and there you are, one dog hooked up and harnessed. After licking the bites and sucking the blood, you tie said dog to a rock and start for the next one. It is only a question of time before you have your team.

When you have them, leave them alone; they must now decide who is fit to be king of the team, and so they fight, they fight and fight; and once they have decided, the king is king. A growl from him, or only a look, is enough, all obey.[6]

Getting the dogs hitched up was only the beginning of the job. The hardest was yet to come—driving them. The Eskimos hitched up their dogs on long rawhide thongs in a fan-shaped formation. And when eight to twelve dogs begin each to go his own way, chaos can result. Direction was achieved only with the mastery of the thirty-foot whip. It was not the pain of the lash that controlled the dogs, but the dogs' knowledge that pain could be inflicted at any moment.

The whip was twenty-eight feet of rawhide sealskin on a two-foot wooden or bone handle. Snapping it was much like casting a fly, but with the speed increased many-fold. The motion was from the elbow, with a quick snap of the wrist, and the final, bulletlike explosion had to occur just above the king dog's ear. At the same time the whip was being cracked, the driver had to grasp the upright handles of the sledge to guide and control it.

Ikwah and Ahnalka were again Henson's tutors, taking him out on the trail day after day. The first effort was inauspicious.

Matt took his place behind the sledge, grasped whip in hand, cried out, "Huk . . . huk," and waited for action. Then he snapped the whip and showered the dogs with snow. As he slashed about them, the dogs wagged their tails and sat down to observe his antics. He cracked the whip again, this time striking Ikwah. Grimly, he gripped the whip handle and lashed out with it again. This time the whip wrapped around his own legs and he fell down. Ikwah and Ahnalka rolled on the snow with him, helpless with laughter.

Within a month, however, Henson was handling a team by himself; by the end of the winter he was almost as good as Ikwah and Ahnalka. He was far better than Peary or any other member of the expedition. But he was not to go on the ice cap. When spring arrived he stayed back at Red Cliff House as servant and companion to Mrs. Peary.

[VI]

Daylight returned with March and the expedition stepped up preparations for the crossing of the great ice cap from western shore to eastern shore and return. Activity brought release from the tensions of the long night and every man threw himself into the work of preparing the equipment. But now a new suspense took over—who would go and who would be left behind?

Peary had let it be known that he considered a small party essential to the success of the long march, and he would take only one man beside himself. Which man? Henson, having been lovingly trained by the Eskimos, was the best dogteam driver. This would seem to make him a prime candidate, at least in the Eskimos' eyes.

Henson's friends and tutors, Ikwah and Ahnalka, summoned him one day and with worried faces led him to a place where they could talk without being overheard.

"Are you going with Pearyaksoah up there?" Ikwah demanded, pointing up the cliffs toward the ice cap.

"I don't know," Henson said. "He hasn't said."

"*Nangia-na-to-voq* (it is dangerous)," Ahnalka burst out.

"Pearyaksoah is well prepared," Henson said.

"No one can be prepared for Kokoyah. He is the devil of the ice cap and he devours all men who come into his place."

Henson said, "*Erk-siniar-nak* (I am not afraid)."

"Miy Paluk," Ikwah said, putting his hand on Henson's arm, "it is not a question of courage, but of wisdom. We Innuits know about the terrible appetite of the devil. You are our brother, so you must also know."

Henson made no answer, for he could think of none. He wanted very much to make the trip with Peary, but he had little real hope of it and he didn't wish to appear ungrateful to his friends for their warning.

The following day Peary summoned him to his private quarters. There was a desk and a bookcase and a curtain to shield the corner bed from the office. Maps of the known land area were spread out and Peary had marked the course of his proposed trip. Once on the ice cap above McCormick Bay he planned to march northeast to the eastern shore of Greenland.

Swinging away from his desk, Peary said, "Matt, we should be under way by the end of April. I plan to send Cook, Gibson, and Astrup on ahead to make caches of food and establish the advance base. You and I will follow a week later and rendezvous with them."

Henson's heart leaped up. He *was* going.

"From the advance camp," Peary continued, "Astrup and I will make the march across the ice cap and the rest of you will return here to Red Cliff House."

Henson's heart fell.

"Your job will be to take care of Mrs. Peary. She will naturally be worried. Keep her spirits up and see no accident befalls her."

Not until this moment did Henson realize how desperately he had wanted to go. All the winter months while he had worked to master the dogteams he had told himself it was for fun and exercise, but now, in the bitterness of his disappointment, he knew it had been to win himself a chance at the trail. He was back where he had started, a servant. With a mental shrug of the shoulders and an inward wry smile, he thought that one good would come of it. Ikwah and Ahnalka could now stop worrying about him.

On April 30 the advance party hitched up their sledges, laboriously climbed the cliff and glacier, and disappeared. On May 3 Peary and Henson harnessed up and followed. The ice they climbed was treacherous, for where it projected down the valley in a long tongue it touched the warming rocks of each side and melted away to leave deep canyons filled with water. The upper surface of the glacier had begun to disintegrate under the reflected heat of the mountains above and, shattered by daily changes of temperature, had become a chaotic labyrinth of crevasses, gullies, and pinnacles. There had recently been drifts of fine, hard snow that extended like a causeway from ice to rock, covering the treacherous gorges beneath.

Henson broke trail, crying, "Huk . . . huk!" to his dogs, snapping the long whip above the king dog's ear, pushing and wrestling his sledge upward over the rocks and onto the glacier. He came to one of the causeways and moved gingerly onto it. Some ice broke beneath his feet and plummeted down to crash echoingly on the jagged rocks below. He thought of Kokoyah, for surely it sounded like the devil's teeth grinding as he waited for him to fall. "Huk . . . huk!" he cried to his team and pushed against the sledge with all his strength. They slid off the causeway and up onto the crest of the dammed-up glacier where the ice lay smoother against the rocks, with less melting.

Now he came to a succession of rounded hummocks, steepest and highest on their land side. Surmounting these, he found the hummocks merging into long swells, slowly flattening as they reached higher toward the interior. By the end of the morning he was on a gently rising plane, and that afternoon it became flat and hard and glazed. They were on the ice cap!

Two marches short of the advance camp where they were to meet the rest of the expedition, a storm swept down upon them. Neither Peary nor Henson knew how to build a snow-block igloo and they were able only to throw up a rudimentary wall of hard-packed snow and huddle together at its base. They slept in sleeping bags, another item they were eventually to learn was unsuited to the trail. The snow covered them and their dogs, and they slept with what body heat they could give each other.

When Henson awoke there was an intense pain in his left eye. He clapped his hand to it, but said nothing. Later, the pain left him and he gave it no more thought, which was just as well as he could have done nothing if he had known the truth. They roused the dogs out of the snow, hitched them up, and were off toward the advance base, making it after one march, a sleep, and a second march.

On May 24 Peary and Astrup left the base, called Camp Separation, and headed northeast. The dogs were fresh and eager, their breaths sending up clouds of steam into the clear, sharp air, their bushy tails wagging. Not many of them were to return. Astrup, the Norwegian ski champion, resolutely wore his native skis despite the fact that they were entirely unsuited to the terrain. Peary wore his ponderous snowshoes, determined not to limp on the leg that had so recently mended. The two men gallantly waved and marched off, growing smaller and smaller on the white landscape and finally disappearing. The rest of the men and the dogs turned back toward Red Cliff House.

The following summer months at Red Cliff House were passed by the men in hunting expeditions. Mrs. Peary was not a hunter, however. She was a fine-boned woman who did not at all like roughing it and whose husband had marched off and left her in the company of men she found, in many ways, quite vulgar. She did what most women do under stress—she cleaned house. And Henson cleaned house. They took out and beat every rug and washed every dish. And when that was done, they beat the rugs and washed the dishes all over again.

Josephine Peary was too proud to reveal directly how worried she was, but Matt knew. She would hardly let him leave her side, and even when she took little camping trips, she demanded that he go with her. Between mistress and servant there were never any words of intimacy; even when their sleeping bags were but inches apart, there was but dependence on her part and loyalty on his. He was ready at all times to stand between her and pain, but of course he could not entirely do this. Her pain came from being married to a man who could give but a small part of himself to her.

Josephine Peary's entries in her journal are revealing. During June she wrote, "Since Matt does the cooking, I take long walks every day and find them most agreeable. We had a general house-cleaning today, and will have it now every Saturday. We have been obliged to dismiss the Eskimos from the living room during mealtime, as their odor is too offensive."

During July she wrote, "I have lived through five days more of intense suspense. The Eskimos console me by talking of Mr. Peary as 'sinnypoh' (dead.)"

And later in her journal the heartbreaking entry: "Never in my life have I felt so utterly alone and forsaken . . . it surely must end sometime."[7]

Henson watched her with increasing concern. She was his responsibility, Peary's last order had been for him to care for her, and yet he knew no way to help her beyond maintaining a cheerful and confident air. She responded gratefully to this, determinedly ignoring the Eskimos who claimed that Kokoyah had certainly eaten up Peary.

During the second week of July she suddenly confronted Henson with a blunt demand. "Matt, I want your honest opinion. When do you think the Lieutenant will return?"

Henson had, of course, no way of knowing. Anything he said would be the wildest guess, yet he realized that even if he was wrong it was better to be positive than vague. Hope was better than honesty. He thought a moment, then said, "I figure they should return during the first week or so of August."

Josephine Peary nodded eagerly. "That was what I had figured." Then she sighed. "But it is difficult just to sit and wait."

"Yes, ma'am, it is. But the time will pass if we keep busy."

"I've kept busy," she said with some impatience.

"Yes, ma'am," Matt said.

Suddenly she squared her small, delicate shoulders and said, "Matt, I'm not going to sit here at Red Cliff House another week. I want to go out and meet Mr. Peary. The two of us will go. You make the arrangements."

"You mean, you want to go out on the ice cap?" Henson asked, unbelieving.

"That's exactly what I mean."

Henson shook his head. "That would be very dangerous. The Lieutenant wouldn't approve of it, not at all. No, ma'am, I'm sorry, but I couldn't do that."

They faced each other, each unyielding, and for a moment she considered *ordering* the servant to obey. But then she gave a small sigh, for she knew he was right.

Seeing the crisis had passed, the test of wills avoided, Henson said, "There's something we might do. We could set up an advance camp at the head of the bay and be there to watch for him on the ice cap. We could be there with a cache of food to greet him the minute he returns."

"Of course!" she exclaimed. "Make the arrangements at once!"

The following week Henson and Ikwah, sledges loaded with provisions, broke trail to establish an advance base at the head of the bay. Two days later Dr. Cook brought Mrs. Peary to camp. Ikwah and Cook returned to Red Cliff House, leaving Henson and Mrs. Peary in their lonely vigil. They kept regular watches around the clock so that one of them would always be awake if Peary appeared out of the vast white desert.

They occupied themselves with hunting trips, with excursions farther and farther inland to lay down caches of food, but no matter how violent the physical activity, Josephine Peary could not entirely down the fear that kept climbing within her. She wrote in her journal, ". . . To offset these dark forebodings and keep my spirits from sinking too low, I repeat a paragraph in Mr. Peary's letter which says: 'I have no doubt I shall be with you August 1st, but if there should be a little delay, it will be delay only, and not danger. I have a hundred days' provisions.'"

On July 24 the *Kite* arrived from the south. An Eskimo took the news to Henson and Mrs. Peary in their advance camp, but she refused to return to Red Cliff House and miss the chance of being the first to greet her returning husband. Finally Professor Angelo Heilprin, chief scientist aboard the relief ship, hiked the fifteen miles to her encampment to plead personally the advantages of her coming aboard the *Kite* while he organized a search party.

She agreed, reluctantly, and entered in her journal, "Professor Heilprin, having determined to move his party to the head of the bay, preparatory to a search on the inland ice, the *Kite* heaved anchor at nine this morning, and is now lying opposite the point which I only recently deserted. By the professor's kind invitation I joined the *Kite* party, and Matt, who has been my steady guardian since Mr. Peary's departure, accompanies me."

That entry was on August 4. On August 5 a rescue party put ashore and started onto the ice cap. On August 6 they saw in the distance two tiny, staggering figures coming down the glacier. They were Peary and Astrup.

Their bearded faces were gray and haggard, their kamiks were worn to shreds, the feet of the few surviving dogs were lacerated and the animals were barely able to drag themselves, let alone the sledges. But in Peary's eyes, bloodshot from attacks of snow-blindness, there burned the fever of victory.

He had traveled a total of 1,200 miles, had discovered a sea on the northeast coast of Greenland and named it Independence Bay. This made *probable* the insularity of the great land mass, but it was not *definite*. In this sense, his victory was a limited one. And this was his goad.

When he came aboard the *Kite* he wrapped his arms around his wife and spoke with some of the wildness of exhaustion. "Next year we'll prove it! Next year we'll explore the eastern coast. This land may be a peninsula that runs all the way north to the Pole. This ice cap may be the imperial highway to the North Pole. Next year we'll come back and pry her secrets from her rocky bosom . . . so help me God!"

Josephine Peary clung to her husband, her head pressed against his gaunt chest. He did not notice her failure to share his enthusiasm: he was too intoxicated with his fatigue and his visions. She had prayed for his return, and her prayers had been answered and she was grateful. But always implicit in her prayers was the hope that he would return freed of the North. Instead, he was more deeply enmeshed than ever. She closed her eyes to conceal the pain of the sudden sure knowledge of what the future was to hold.

Standing nearby on the deck of the *Kite*, Henson saw and understood and felt compassion. Still, his tender emotion was all but overwhelmed by a feeling of elation. They were coming back! He would again hunt and laugh with his Eskimo friends. Maybe this next time he would even get on the trail with the lieutenant.

Henson, no less than Peary, was caught by the North.

[VII]

Before the *Kite* sailed for home, John Verhoeff, the mineralogist, asked permission to make a final trip overland to the Eskimo settlements in Robertson Bay for the purpose of collecting specimens. Peary was reluctant to let him go alone, but finally gave permission.

Two days passed, the allotted time, and Verhoeff did not return. Peary at once undertook extensive searches, throwing the entire expedition into the operation. Ikwah and Henson headed up one party that included Gibson and several Eskimos. Four days had passed since Verhoeff's disappearance and the search party double-marched back and forth over the Robertson Bay glacier.

Ikwah, breaking trail, suddenly halted his sledge and motioned the others behind him to approach carefully. Henson came up to find an imprint of a snowshoe next to a gaping hole that led hundreds of feet down into a black canyon on whose floor was a forest of jagged rocks. The track could only belong to Verhoeff. He had plunged to his death through the thin ice that insidiously concealed the abyss.

Ikwah said, "*Kokoyah eat kabloona* (the devil has eaten the white man)." He had long predicted Kokoyah's anger at the penetration of his domain, and here was the proof. There was some satisfaction in his voice, as there is bound to be when a man finds the world properly ordered after all.

During the voyage homeward Peary entered into his journal a judgment of the men of his expedition:

> To Dr. Cook's care may be attributed the almost complete exemption of the party from even the mildest indispositions and personally I owe much to his professional skill, and unruffled patience and coolness in an emergency. In addition to his work in his special ethnological field, in which he has obtained a large mass of most valuable material concerning a practically unstudied tribe, he was always helpful and an indefatigable worker.
>
> Verhoeff, besides contributing generously to the expense of the expedition, was devoted to his meteorological and tidal observations and made a complete and valuable series of both.
>
> Gibson, a natural hunter, quick with rifle and gun, in addition to his ornithological work, contributed more largely than any other member to our supply of game.
>
> Astrup, a young Norwegian, a boy in years, but a man in grit and endurance, was one among a thousand for the long and lonely journey during which he was my sole companion.
>
> Henson, my faithful colored boy, a hard worker and apt at anything, being in turn cook, hunter, dog driver, housekeeper, and bodyguard, showed himself, in powers of endurance and ability to withstand cold, the equal of others in the party.[8]

They were generous words from a leader who, flushed with success and eager for the next foray, had forgotten the tensions that had riven these men during the long Arctic night. He did not at this time know that only two of them (Astrup and Henson) would go north with him the next trip, and only one (Henson) would stay with him after that.

When the *Kite* returned home the members of the expedition found themselves welcomed as heroes. The average American didn't quite know what they had accomplished, but was aware that the nation's prestige had been greatly enhanced. Russia,

Great Britain, and the Scandinavian countries had all been probing the North, and generally with greater success than the
Americans. The last official expedition the United States had sent
north was in 1881, a project conceived and carried out by the
Army and under the command of Major Adolphus W. Greely.
It was a success only in the heroism of the men. The band of
soldiers survived on seaweed and their own clothing until the
spring of 1884 when they began to die of starvation one at a
time. When the relief ship smashed through Melville Bay and
rounded Cape Sabine, it found a pitiful seven men left out of the
original company of twenty-five.

But now Peary, a man little known, appeared with dramatic
suddenness as the champion of American aspirations in the North,
and the public thrilled to his success, and to his promises of
greater things to come. Little was noted about Matthew Henson.
If reference was made to him in the spate of feature stories it was
only to identify him as "Peary's colored servant."

Upon returning to New York, Henson received the fifty dollars
due him under the contract, and he was on his own until the next
expedition could be organized by Peary. This didn't worry him—
there was always work available, the menial and abundant work
open to a colored boy—but now his eye began to pain him again.
He looked up Dr. Cook, who was in Philadelphia.

After examining him Cook leaned back in his chair and said
candidly, "Matt, it's beyond me. Obviously you froze that eyeball
on the trail and now there are some complications. But it's for
an ophthalmologist, a specialist. I can send you to a good man.
It may mean hospitalization, though."

"I don't know as I can afford that, Doc," Henson said.

"Oh? Tell me, Matt, how much money do you have?"

"About thirty dollars left, I guess."

"Thirty dollars! Good Lord, how much were you paid?"

"Fifty dollars."

Cook looked at him, unbelieving. "You mean, for the entire
year?"

Henson grinned. "It's fifty dollars more than you were paid, Doc."

Cook laughed and said, "You're right there, but . . ." He thought better of the sentence and didn't finish it. What he was going to say was that he went north as an explorer, not as a servant. Instead, he said, "We'll have to work something out, Matt. You need treatment."

Cook generously paid Henson's fare to Brooklyn and put him up in his mother's home. Dr. Jackson M. Mills examined Matt and discovered a severe case of sun-blindness. This was something both Henson and Peary were to suffer from periodically in the coming decades in the North. It is caused by the presence in the Arctic of intense ultraviolet and actinic rays. The actinic ray is a property of radiant energy found in the shorter wave lengths, and both rays are outside the visible spectrum.

These rays had produced tiny blisters on the cornea of Henson's eye. Some of the blisters had broken open, becoming ulcerous and causing extreme pain when the eye opened and closed.

The doctor's treatment was given without charge, and for the two months Henson was confined in bed, Cook's sister Lilly was his nurse. His eyes responded well, and by December, 1892, he was ready to leave the family to whom he would be forever grateful. Dr. Cook came to visit his mother the week Henson was to leave, and received the profuse thanks in a preoccupied manner. It was obvious that he had something on his mind, and finally it came out.

"Matt, have you heard from Peary recently?"

"Yes, I have. He's organizing a lecture tour."

"I know, I know," Cook muttered darkly.

"He asked me to go on it with him. He wants to use the team of dogs he brought back and I guess he wants me to handle the dogs, get them onto the platform and off without any fights breaking out."

"I've put together a lecture, too," Cook said. "It's based on the ethnological material I gathered about the Eskimos. You remember all those pictures and measurements we took? There's a lot of interest in them, but now suddenly Peary refuses to let me lecture. I've talked to him several times about it, but he absolutely refuses."

Henson thought a moment. "Wasn't it in your contract that you couldn't lecture or write about the expedition for two years?"

"Heck, I thought that was just a formality. I had no idea he'd hold us to it. It's unfair, you know. He goes out to lecture but won't let me. He just wants everything for himself. Well, one thing is certain, I've gone north with him for the last time. After this it will be on my own."

It was not quite true that Peary wanted everything for himself, as Cook charged, but he did want everything for his *work*. He conceived of himself as an instrument of America's destiny in the North, and was fully convinced that anything done to advance himself in this great work was not only moral and just but patriotic. Being a man without any funds of his own, he was faced with a stiff battle to finance his expeditions and he knew that his writings and lecturing would be a vital source of income. Every cent he made, beyond modest living expenses, went into his expeditions right up to the last one. He expected Cook, and everyone else connected with any of his expeditions, to share this Spartan dedication to his mission.

The lecture tour Henson had referred to was actually undertaken reluctantly and at the last minute. Up until the winter of 1893 Peary had hoped that scientific organizations would entirely underwrite his second Greenland expedition, but this didn't happen. Money was forthcoming, but not fast enough to suit Peary, and he decided upon the expedient of the lecture tour. With Henson, he put together a performance that was a smashing success. Among his other qualities was a sense of drama.

The curtain parted to reveal an Eskimo village complete with tupik (tent), sledges, weapons, and furs in great quantities. No one had ever seen such things, and they immediately set a mood of mystery and adventure. Then onto the stage strode Peary, dressed in Arctic furs. He was tall, handsome, masterful, all that the audience dreamed an explorer would be. If his lecture was rather wooden in delivery, the stories he told them were thrilling. The climax of the performance came when suddenly the audience heard from the wings the strange cry, "Huk . . . huk . . . huk!" immediately followed by the report of a cracking whip. Onto the stage raced eight Eskimo dogs driven by Henson, complete in Eskimo garb. A cry of astonishment went up from the audience, followed by involuntary applause.

Henson had trained the dogs so that after their boisterous entrance they sat quietly while Peary continued the lecture. However, the moment Peary exceeded his allotted time they lost their patience and set up a howl, thereby ending the performance amid laughter and good cheer all around.

In 103 days Peary and Henson made 165 appearances. The tour brought in the sum of $20,000, of which $13,000 went to the expedition. This, combined with monies privately and institutionally contributed, was sufficient to get the expedition under way. The *Falcon* sailed out of Philadelphia on June 23, 1893.

The dimension of the party had grown considerably. It included the following: Samuel Entrikin, Eivind Astrup, Edward Vincent, surgeon, E. B. Baldwin, meteorologist, George H. Clark, taxidermist, Hugh J. Lee, George H. Carr, James Davidson, Walter F. Swain, Frederick Stokes, artist, Mrs. Susan J. Cross, nurse, Mrs. Peary, and Matthew Henson.

Later Peary was to write: "Carried away by enthusiasm, and with no time in the rapid whirl of effort for a calm consideration of the matter, I made the fatal mistake of taking, contrary to my expressed theory, a large party."[9]

This was an understatement to the extreme! It was not only a large party, but one unsuited by training and temperament to perform the tasks allotted to it. If there had been tensions in the previous expedition, this one almost came apart at the seams.

To begin with, Mrs. Peary was pregnant! The child was due some time during September, right at the moment the long Arctic night and winter storms would descend. It was, no doubt, heroic of Josephine Peary to face her ordeal under such terrible conditions, but her heroism was vastly to complicate life for the other members of the expedition.

Henson was among the first to learn of the impending event. Peary said to him, "Matt, Mrs. Peary is going to have a baby during the expedition."

"Congratulations, sir," Matt said, after recovering from surprise.

"Thank you, thank you," Peary said beaming. "September, the doctor thinks. Now, I'm counting on you to look after Mrs. Peary. Oh, there'll be a doctor present, of course, and Mrs. Cross, the nurse—they'll take care of all the medical aspects—but you must see that Mrs. Peary's other needs are always met. And when the baby comes, you protect it just as if it were your own."

"Yes, sir," Matt said, concealing his disappointment. Now he was to be nursemaid to a baby! The chance of going on the trail seemed more remote than ever before.

Peary mused, "This child of mine will be the first white child born in the Far North, the first American born north of the Arctic Circle."

The *Falcon* steamed north by the same route taken by the *Kite* the year before, but this time deposited the expedition at Bowdoin Bay just south of McCormick Bay. The new house, large because of the expanded expedition and the imminent birth, was called Anniversary Lodge, for it was on this site that Peary and his wife had stood during their wedding anniversary the previous year. The *Falcon* sailed for home on August 20, with the house still unfinished.

A warm reunion took place between Henson and his old Eskimo friends who flocked back to assist the new expedition. Hunting parties were undertaken to supply seal and walrus and reindeer meat; other expeditions were sent onto the ice to lay down caches of food; but the one overshadowing event was the coming birth of the baby. In a partitioned-off corner of the Lodge, Mrs. Peary lay in labor. And on September 12, 1893, she delivered a nine-pound baby girl who was named Marie Ahnighito

Peary, and was dubbed the Snow Baby. Eskimos came from miles around to look with amazement on the tiny white face, and to touch it with their brown fingers to make certain it was flesh and not snow.

As soon as they were able, mother and child were taken outdoors and posed for a picture. The baby was wrapped, not in blankets, not in furs, but in an American flag!

[VIII]

Aside from the safe arrival of the Snow Baby, nothing seemed to go right. Peary had brought north a pack of burros, hoping to use them to supplement dog power, but one by one they sickened and died. Astrup was sent up on the ice cap to lay down supplies, but was caught in severe storms and couldn't carry out the assignment. Then he became ill and was of little use for many weeks. Carr had fallen on the ice and injured his back. A freak gigantic wave came out of the bay to attack the Lodge and smash most of the barrels of oil needed for winter fuel. In February, Lee, who had been laying down caches on the moraine, from which point the crossing of the ice cap was to begin, got caught in a storm and after forty-eight hours staggered into camp with a frozen toe.

An indication of how low the morale of the expedition had fallen was the fact that even Henson became involved in a controversy. It was with the buxom and bumptious Mrs. Cross. She had been brought north as a nurse, but the Pearys had assumed she would share general housekeeping chores when not actually engaged in nursing. She resented this as beneath her professional dignity and demanded that Henson do the menial work. Henson, frustrated in his desire to be on the trail, resented and ignored her orders to him. The mood in Anniversary Lodge was not a happy one.

During the first week of March, 1894, Peary set out on his projected sledging expedition with a party of eight: Entrikin, Clark, Davidson, Lee, Carr, Astrup, and Dr. Vincent. His plan was to cross the ice cap to Independence Bay and there divide into three parties. One party of three would proceed northward along the coast in hope of advancing well toward the North Pole. A second party of three would follow the coast southward to Cape Bismarck and then return across the ice cap to base. The other two men would remain at Independence Bay and hunt for food, laying in provisions for themselves and the returning northern party.

It didn't work out as planned. Frostbite and storms put members out of operation one by one and they had to be sent back to the Lodge. Peary kept on with an ever diminishing party but sledges broke, sleeping bags became heavy with moisture and almost unportable, and strange mirages began to destroy their nerves. Peary wrote: " . . . the winter and temperature, acting upon the moisture of Baldwin's breath, froze his kooletah [fur jacket] so rigid that he could neither walk nor turn his head, and was obliged to come into camp lying on his sledge."[10]

One of the dogs came down with piblokto, a little-understood disease that attacked both animals and humans. It frequently appeared among the Eskimo women during the winter nights and took the form of hysterical screaming and running, usually accompanied by the stripping off of their clothes and jumping into the freezing waters. When forcibly restrained, the seizure would pass and the woman become as cheerful and tractable as before. The dogs, on the other hand, failed to recover when stricken by piblokto. The madness made them attack and bite everything within reach and, being a menace to the rest of the pack, they were always killed by the driver. Piblokto was dreaded on the trail because its appearance meant cruel reductions in the size of the teams. In this case, the first appearance of the madness among the dogs came on April 10 and the expedition was only 128 miles out from the Lodge.

Peary wrote a report of the party's condition: ". . . one [man] was entirely out of the race with frosted feet, and must return to the Lodge. Another was not entirely recovered from an attack of cramps at the last camp, and I feared another storm would bring them on again. The third had both heels and great toes frost-bitten, and was having daily attacks of bleeding from the nose. . . . "[11]

On top of the disintegration of his men, there was the serious problem of the lateness of the season. He had planned to be at Independence Bay on April 1, but here it was the 10th and he was only a quarter of the way. With heavy heart Peary gave the signal to turn back. On the return trip he carefully cached his supplies, marking each with tall poles in case drifts covered them. Thus would food be available for his next trip across the ice cap.

While Peary and his band were freezing on the ice cap, an event took place back in camp that was to have ironic overtones. One afternoon the redoubtable Mrs. Cross looked up from the preparation of baby Marie's food to find Matt Henson standing before her. On his face was an expression both apologetic and defiant. Beside him stood a small Eskimo boy, his tiny hand gripping Matt's large forefinger.

"I want to heat some water," Henson said.

"What for?" Mrs. Cross demanded suspiciously.

"I'm going to give him a bath."

She looked down at the child with matted hair and shabby, dirt-streaked clothing. "Not in this kitchen!" she announced.

Henson put a bucket of water on the oil stove, saying, "Certainly not outdoors, Mrs. Cross."

"Now see here, Matt, we can't have these filthy little heathens running all over the place."

Henson lit the fire. "He won't be filthy after I bathe him."

"I'll see Mrs. Peary about this," stormed Mrs. Cross. "You can't bring every stray into this kitchen."

Henson swung around to face her, then said quietly, "He's not a stray, Mrs. Cross. He's my son. His name is Kudlooktoo."

She gasped and retreated a step, her hand protectively to her bosom. She had heard stories about the sinful goings-on in the igloos, but this was the first time she had come face to face with the consequences.

Henson couldn't keep a grin from his face. "He's an orphan, Mrs. Cross, and I've adopted him."

This put a slightly different light on it. Still it was too much for Mrs. Cross and she fled to the private quarters occupied by Mrs. Peary and the baby, there to tell her woes. Henson cut the boy's hair short, stripped off his greasy clothes and burned them, then scrubbed the small brown body until it glowed a glistening copper. Fresh furs were put on the child, who through it all had remained stoic and silent.

"*Agga-nik tigu-lau-langa* (give me your hand)," Matt said to him. The child trustingly slipped his tiny fist into the big, hard one and was led into the other room. Matt spread furs on the floor beneath his own bunk and put the child to bed. On his hands and knees, he rubbed the little turned-up nose with his own and murmured, "*Sinnit-si-arit* (sleep well)."

The child smiled happily and closed his eyes.

In the days that followed, wherever Henson went, little Kudlooktoo went. And on the round little brown face was an expression of unutterable hero-worship and love.

It was highly significant that Henson had been allowed to adopt the child. The Eskimos cherished children and when Kudlooktoo's widowed mother died, all the neighbors expressed eagerness to take the child. Yet when Henson expressed his own interest, all gave way to him. The tribe would not have done this for anybody but Henson.

The irony of all this was that at the very moment Henson had symbolically become an Eskimo (by fatherhood), Peary and his men on the ice cap were freezing because they did not know enough of Eskimo ways.

The *Falcon* was due to come north in August, and Peary was aghast at the idea of returning on her, defeated. He conferred with Henson on the problem.

"Matt, I'm going to stay through the winter and make another try next spring. How do you feel about it?"

"I'll stay," Matt said at once.

"Good boy." Peary grinned. "I was sure you would. Now, our principal problem is one of supplies. We have food caches along the trail, which will help take care of the expedition next spring, but we'll have to depend on local game to see us through the winter here at the Lodge. Expecting us to return, the *Falcon* will not bring new provisions north and so it will be up to us to eat off the land."

"There should be plenty of reindeer this fall," Matt said.

"Even so, we'll have a smaller party. I'll ask for volunteers and then pick the three best men. We can eliminate a lot of dead wood that way."

Hugh Lee, the young newspaperman from Meriden, Connecticut, wrote his mother a letter dated April 27, 1895, in which he said:

. . . Last evening Mr. Peary had a talk with the party and told us that the party had not failed, that when it came near time for the ship to come he would call for volunteers and from those who volunteered he would choose three. . . . Those three would remain with him another year and the rest come home. As I feel now I would volunteer and perhaps be chosen as one of the three. . . . What would be the advantages of remaining another year (?). First, there would be but four who would live together. Mr. Peary would not be in a separate place. . . . Then, we would have a great deal of experience and could have much better outfits than we have had this year—there would be but four and so the resources would be more in proportion to the number.[12]

When Peary mentioned volunteers, he did not require an answer at once; the men had ample time to think it over before the ship arrived. Then, unable to stand inactivity, he took Matt sledging south down the coast of Greenland in search of the giant meteorites discovered by Sir Joseph Ross in 1818. He found the meteorites, made careful note of their location, and returned to the Lodge only a few days before the arrival of the *Falcon*.

He was now ready to receive volunteers. But none came forward. Though he didn't press any man—there was a week yet—he couldn't help wondering what was going on in their minds. He now felt the lonely burden of leadership.

Peary was a special kind of leader. He was not the born leader in the sense that he could inflame men to heroic deeds: he had no hypnotic charm that could momentarily make weak men into strong ones. He did not dispense lavish praise or make glowing promises. He was often abrupt in manner, always demanding in work, utterly scornful of whiners and malingerers. What he did possess was a high and unswerving sense of justice. If a man did a good job he was praised; if he did a poor one he was criticized. No man was asked to undertake more than Peary himself would do. In short, he was a good leader of strong men. Lesser men often found him intolerable.

The *Falcon* hove to in Melville Bay on August 3; she would sail on the 23rd. Mrs. Cross had already announced she had had enough and was going back, which meant that Mrs. Peary and the baby would have to go. Astrup had had a physical breakdown, Carr a frozen foot, Davidson a wrenched back. Still, there *were* able-bodied men, but they looked the other way. Finally, at the last minute there was one volunteer. It was Hugh J. Lee.

Lee recorded the event in his diary:

He [Peary] told me he had asked each of the others if he would stay another year and each had refused. Then he told me that Matt would stay and asked, "How about you?"

I replied, "I'll stay with you."

With a look of joy he said, "Do you mean it?" and I said, "Sure."

"Do you *really* mean it?" he asked, and when I assured him I did, he said, "Well, shake hands on it."[13]

When it came time for the *Falcon* to sail, Peary and Henson and five Eskimos went down the bay with her in a whaleboat. Good-bys were waved from small boat to large at the last moment as the *Falcon* turned south through Melville Bay. Of all those who lined the rail of the steamer, only Mrs. Peary felt any reluctance to go, and her tie was not to the bleak land but to the man who stood in the stern of the whaleboat. He waved and shouted last-minute endearments and she smiled bravely back, concealing the bitterness within her.

She never did reveal to him how she felt that day, or at the many other moments of separation over the years to come. Not until the baby in her arms had grown to womanhood did she ever confess her heart. "Mother," Marie Peary said to her years later, "how did you really feel about Father spending all those years in the North?"

The little old woman, handsome still, and proud, gave her daughter a searching look, then countered with a question of her own. "How would you like to share your husband with a mistress? The Arctic was your father's mistress. I could never stand against her."

At the moment of leavetaking back in Melville Bay, Peary was experiencing some bitterness, too. His was not directed at his wife, but at the other members of the expedition. He later wrote: " . . . the *Falcon* steamed south with everyone else on board. Davidson and Carr were invalided, the former with a frosted heel and the latter with a weak back; the other members of my party had discovered that Arctic work was not entirely the picnic they had imagined, and wisely regarding discretion as the better part of valor, had decided to return home; Lee and Henson alone possessed the grit and loyalty to remain."[14]

Peary's command had shrunk to two men.

[IX]

As the *Falcon* turned south and the whaleboat turned north, Matthew Henson was the only completely happy man on the scene. He had no wife to worry about and divide his loyalties. What family he had was here in the North in the body of Kudlooktoo. There was nothing to alloy his excitement over the coming adventure. He joked with the five Eskimos who made up the boat crew. There were Kardah, known as "three-ply" because of his habit of repeating everything three times, Ingopahdo or "freckles" because of his splotched complexion, quiet and hardworking Kahdahsu, round-faced and merry Akpudisoahho, and plodding but faithful Nooktah. They all responded to Henson's ebullience, making jokes and laughing.

The whaleboat was grandly named *General Wistar*, and she was nearly 200 miles south of the Lodge at Bowdoin Bay. There were treacherous waters and uncertain weather to be navigated and her motive power was a small sail and seven pairs of human arms. As she started bravely north along the coast, Peary began to discuss the winter plans with Henson, asking his advice on a number of points. There was a new mood of comradeship between them.

They discussed the food problem first. At the Lodge, where

Lee waited, there was sufficient food for the winter with the exception of meat. It was decided that Henson and the Eskimos would go to the deer pastures to get meat for the men, and then to the walrus feeding grounds to obtain dog food. While this was being done, Peary and Lee would go out on the ice cap to locate the caches of food and re-mark them so they could be easily found during the spring march.

The winter could be spent in leisurely repair of equipment and clothes, in practice sledge trips, in toning up the minds and bodies for the extreme physical tests of the spring march. There was only one problem that worried Peary: the possibility of an epidemic of piblokto ravaging the dog pack. If it did break out, they might not have enough dogs left in the spring to make the march. Peary discussed it with Henson; Henson then discussed it with the Eskimos. Peary could speak a pidgin sort of Eskimo but couldn't come near Henson's fluency.

After a lengthy discussion, Henson reported back to Peary, "They're not much help. They say there is no way of knowing when piblokto might break out, no symptoms to watch for, no cure. They say it is the work of the devil. And—" he laughed ruefully—"they say that since we have already offended the devil by going onto the ice cap, he might well send piblokto to our dogs to prevent us from doing it again."

"Humph!" snorted Peary, frowning ahead at the darkening sea. "Tell them to lay on those oars."

"Huk . . . huk!" Henson called to the Eskimos. Since this was the order given to dogs on the trail, it was very funny and everyone had to double over with laughter. It was several moments before the Eskimos had recovered sufficiently to obey the command.

Peary, always conscious of the drama about him, entered in his journal: "As I turned . . . northward towards the gloom of the coming Arctic night, for which my boat was heading, my eyes rested upon my Eskimo crew, pulling with all the strength of their iron-muscled backs for the shelter of the bleak rocks of Cape Athol. A strange, wild, fur-clad crew. . . . With an American leader, an African coxswain, and an Eskimo crew, I had the Equator, the Temperate Zone and the Pole, all compressed into a space of twenty-eight feet."[15]

Savage storms were frequent in these waters at this time of year, and Peary looked anxiously at the froth being whipped up on the waves. Flakes of snow were beginning to descend from an opaque sky. The *General Wistar* was not built to withstand the kind of weather that seemed in the making and Peary nudged Henson, who nodded his head and called out for a faster stroke on the oars.

The Eskimos bent to their work, but did not let it interfere with their conversation. They were garrulous as so many sparrows, swapping spicy gossip about the tribe, talking about the wonderful ship they had just seen, reviewing incidents of the trip they were on, talking to the sky and the waves and the birds. An inquisitive gull swooped low over the boat and they all laughed happily and shouted advice. A flock of bustling little auks flew by and they were cheered on with cries of, "Go it, little ones . . . you'll get there . . . don't get tired." When a seal raised his head out of the waters there was the cry, *"Taku! Taku-u-u* (Look . . . look)!" One would have thought this was the first seal they had seen in their lives.

They were ebullient, irrepressible, childlike. If the weather turned bad, they would then cope with it; they did not propose to worry in advance. Let the white man worry, if he wished. Worry seemed to be the disease of his race.

Peary broke out the sail and under the stiff, offshore breeze they made Cape Athol at 1:30 P.M. After a brief reconnoiter ashore, they saw the tides were loosening the ice pan, allowing them to beat their way farther up the coast. Alternately sailing, rowing, camping on the shore to hunt and eat and sleep, they made their tortuous way northward until they came to the glittering Misumisu, the largest iceberg-forming glacier along this shore.

It was an ice stream that, over decades and decades, had flowed down from the ice cap, down a gorge, and projected a good

300 yards into the sea. About midway from shore to its face was a magnificent tunnel large enough to span a ten-story building. The *General Wistar* could either sail through the tunnel or laboriously beat her way out to sea and sail around the iceberg and into the more violent water of the open sound. Under Peary's order, Henson steered the boat toward the tunnel. There was little wind here and the Eskimos bent their backs to the oars as the great arch loomed above them. The air between the vaulting crystal roof and the liquid floor was a shimmering blue and it seemed as if they were about to enter some enchanted world.

The bow of the whaleboat was just about to enter the tunnel when there came a strange sound above their heads, like a celestial explosion, like the heavens cracking open. Henson looked up and gasped. It was as if a piece of the sky was falling!

An enormous block of ice had broken loose from the keystone of the arch and was hurtling downward. It fell with a roar into the water floor of the tunnel, sending out peals of thunder and a great wave which attacked and shook the tiny boat, threatening to capsize it. Henson put the tiller hard over and yelled at the Eskimos. They needed no urging as they bent the oars in a mighty effort to escape.

The falling of the ice block was the signal for the general disintegration of the glacier's face. Fragment after fragment fell outwards, buttress after buttress toppled, until the entire face of the glacier was hidden in a hissing fury of spray, out of which raced angry waves to catch the fleeing boat.

Tossed and bruised, gasping and wet, they made the safety of the sound and raised the sail to assist their aching arms. When they were miles away they could still hear the reports of the rending ice and the muffled roar of the waves hurling themselves into the newly formed caverns.

On the evening of the second day they put ashore, beached and overturned the *General Wistar*, then made camp in a sheltered cove. Food was now a problem and on the morning of the third day the Eskimos took off along the coast to hunt. The weather looked promising for a time; the snow had stopped and the wind died down, and both Peary and Henson sat in the lee of the up-turned *General Wistar*, talking quietly of their coming winter plans. The sky was a strange metallic color, leaden, but seemingly without menace.

Then it happened! Almost without warning the two men were in the midst of an Anoahtaksoah, a peculiarly vicious sort of storm referred to by the Eskimos as the Demon of the Great Ice.

These storms are caused by a sudden imbalance of the atmosphere, a tilting of it, almost. A section of cold, heavy air existing above the interior ice cap suddenly starts to move toward the nearest exit point on the coast. It moves down the incline of the cap, gravity constantly accelerating it, until it finds a fjord and plunges, roaring, into it. It carries its heavy burden of snow hissing and screaming into the sea. It constitutes a gigantic air-jet which can move all but the heaviest objects.

This was what now vented itself upon Peary and Henson. They huddled in a cove, the only sheltered spot in the entire bay, but still the wind clawed at them, shook them.

"Matt, the boat!" Peary suddenly cried, pointing.

The wind snatched the words out of his mouth and blew them away, but Henson turned to follow the pointing finger and saw, in horror, the bow of the *General Wistar* beginning to lift. The whaleboat had been beached upside down, and heavy as she was, she now began to flutter like a chip of wood. If the storm increased, the boat would be blown into the sea and lost. As they tried to decide what to do, the boat upended, stood quiveringly erect for a moment, then smashed back down. Even without going into the sea she could be pounded to pieces.

With one accord, Peary and Henson jumped up and ran for the boat. The moment they stepped out of the protection of the cove they were knocked flat. They tried to rise and were knocked flat again, the giant hand of the storm pressing hard on their backs. They began to crawl, animal-like. Stones cut their hands and the storm pulled the breath from their mouths, but they inched forward, coming nearer and nearer the trembling boat.

At last they made it and, with the strength of desperation, they piled rocks on the boat's stern. Then they passed a grapnel rope across the bow and weighted it down on each side with stones. This seemed to hold the *General Wistar* against the beach and they began their tortuous trip back to the shelter of the cove. The storm had increased and was now picking up rocks and flinging them at them. They advanced, as under a bombardment, dodging the larger boulders, helplessly taking the smaller ones on their shoulders and backs. With the last of their waning strength they made the cove.

That afternoon the storm seemed to abate a bit, but the wind was still too strong to stand against. Now a new danger crept upon them. Imperceptibly the tide began to come in. They were not aware of its significance at first, but suddenly they saw the tide accomplish what the wind had failed to do—lift the boat, rocks and all. High and higher the tide rolled in toward the cove, sweeping the boat before it. Henson and Peary grabbed up a sail-sprit and fended the boat off the rocks. They took turns, each man working to the limit of his strength, then returning to the task when the other faltered.

When it seemed they were about to be defeated, when exhaustion of mind and body reached the point where the boat hardly seemed worth saving, the storm abated. The *General Wistar* settled in her fetters quite innocently, as if she had never caused them a moment's concern.

Late that night the hunters returned bearing slaughtered reindeer. They heard with surprise the story of the Anoahtaksoah. They had been only a few miles off and it had not touched them. The Eskimos looked wise and murmured to each other that it was the work of the devil, of Kokoyah.

The trip up the coast was resumed only to have yet another danger threaten them. The season was well advanced and the sound was beginning to freeze over. It became more and more difficult to find leads of open water through which to sail and row the *General Wistar*. Every day, every hour, was of great importance, and no time could be wasted in sleep.

One day was made memorable by the appearance of a school of narwhal, the fabled sea unicorn. Ingopahdo was in the bow of the boat and spotted them just to starboard. He called out in a stage whisper to the rest of the crew and all of them shipped oars to let the boat move forward silently. These are the most timid of mammals, and though their ears are the size of a pencil point, their hearing is extremely good. On this day, for some mysterious reason, they did not fear or resent the intrusion of the *General Wistar*. They moved alongside the boat, now sunning themselves, their dark spotted backs just afloat, now playing, swimming from open pool to open pool and surfacing to breathe, their wet ivory tusks glistening. They breathe through a hole in the top of their heads, as does a porpoise.

The narwhal averages twenty feet in length and its horn, or tusk, is a development of one of its upper left canine teeth. It grows and grows, protruding through the upper lip just to the left of the nose. It is straight as a lance, spiraled from right to left, and has been known to reach a length of nine feet.

Whereas swordfish have been known to use their horns to attack other fish, and even the bottoms of fishing boats, the narwhal horn has never been used in anger. Sometimes two of them will playfully fence with their horns, but beyond that it is an ornament.

All this lore was excitedly imparted to Henson and Peary by the Eskimos. They also reported that the meat is black in color and even more oily in taste than seal. The Eskimo custom was to dry it by hanging it on the face of a cliff. It was served as a delicacy to visitors during the winter.

Peary forbade taking any narwhal at this time, for he was determined to carry no more weight during the arduous trip remaining before them. Sadly the Eskimos watched the narwhal gambol in pools farther and farther distant, and then disappear.

At last they came to Bowdoin Bay and set their course across it toward the Lodge on the opposite shore. But the bay was a chaos of trash ice and icebergs and large fields of last winter's ice, all cemented together by the young ice just forming. There was

practically no open water at all and it took the most strenuous
effort to force the boat forward. After six hours they made land
at a point five miles from the Lodge. They hauled the boat ashore,
secured her, and hiked the rest of the way.

Hugh Lee was sitting in the Lodge, writing a letter home by
candlelight. He was homesick and glad they had returned.

[X]

The coming winter was to alter both Peary and Henson, and to forge a new relationship between them. They had been together for eight years: Peary was now thirty-eight and Henson twenty-eight. They had known adventure and hardship and frustration, but always they had been separated by the conventions of master and servant. This was now largely to disappear. Peary was not particularly eager for the new intimacy; events forced it. In two expeditions to Greenland he had had sixteen different men under his command, not counting ships' crews, and all of them had failed, in one way or another, to measure up to his expectations. All save Henson. There was Hugh Lee, of course, but for all the great courage he was to show during the coming marches, he was a boy, a tenderfoot, and he had neither Henson's knowledge of the North nor his strength to combat it.

Of the many factors forcing the new comradeship between Peary and Henson, the Eskimos were the greatest. Peary had come north with an arrogance of race and culture; he had written that it is the educated man who is most resilient under pressure, who survives and succeeds because he is able to *will* his survival and success. But the North was teaching him some modesty. The Eskimos, people of the Stone Age, not only survived here but prospered. More and more he was employing their techniques, and in the end, it was the total adoption of their way of travel and dress and living that made possible his discovery of the Pole.

Henson was his bridge to these aborigines. The Eskimos respected and trusted Peary, but they loved Henson. And in their primitive society more things were done for love than for duty.

Following their arrival at Anniversary Lodge, Peary and Henson rested a few days and then began preparations for the winter. Henson and Ahnalka headed a party of Eskimos that went off to the caribou-grazing area. A week later they returned with six carcasses. Peary and Lee led a party on a walrus hunt in the *General Wistar*. They returned with the boat filled to the gunwales with these monsters. Men and dogs would be supplied with meat through the winter.

The slaughter of the walrus greatly impressed the Eskimos, for these were fierce and strong beasts. When an Eskimo killed one, he was honored by his friends at a feast, and now the tradition held.

"Pearyaksoah is a great hunter," Ahnalka said to Henson after the walrus had been removed from the boat, quartered, and hung up to freeze.

"Great hunter," Henson agreed.

"We will have a feast for him. Come to my igloo."

Henson carried the invitation to Peary. Subtly Henson tried to make it clear that this was a command invitation, for it was important not to flout any of the Eskimo traditions. Peary, Lee, and Henson went to Ahnalka's igloo that evening. It was already crowded with the host's friends and relatives, but they made room for the honored newcomers. Peary wrote of that evening:

. . . a walrus head . . . [was] the *pièce de résistance* of the evening's feast. Placed in the midst of the eager group, one would carve lumps from the thick, gelatinous lips, another slice the rich tongue, another gouge an eye and, puncturing it with his knife, suck it as we suck the pulp from a grapeskin, while another, with a deftly shaped bit of board, would extract the exquisite omelette of the brain, till finally the massive skull would be left as bare and white as if cleaned by ants or shrimps.

. . . I doubt if Dante or Doré could have done justice to the scene: The air heavy with the peculiar flabby-musky odour of the lifeless yet fresh walrus blood and flesh; the glowing stove, the sullen red eye of the quintessence of all evil, filling the room with blood-shot gloom, through which showed the blood-smeared faces, white teeth, and glittering eyes of the group of fur-clad demons quarrelling over the massive skull; while from the background, hideous, mis-shapen deformities of webbed hands reached out for them; and from above, heavily mustached faces, with white-fanged mouths, glared at them.[16]

How differently Henson would have written of this banquet. He would have told of the laughter and jokes, the warm fellow-ship, the generous honor being done the great hunter.

At the beginning of October, Peary, Henson, and Lee began a series of excursions onto the ice cap with the purpose of locating and re-marking their food caches to feed them during the spring march. The trip was a failure and dealt a shattering blow to their morale. They couldn't find the caches because they had been covered with snow. Desperately they quartered every inch of the cap where the caches had been, and searched for the tall poles that had been left as markers.

Then, at last, they found one! It was not a six-foot pole; it was six inches! The cache was buried and frozen beyond re-covery. All the essential supplies for the spring expedition were gone!

The three men were dazed by the loss and returned to the Lodge with dragging steps. Peary wrote:

The sole result of nine days of wasted time and effort had been to satisfy me beyond a doubt that all my essential supplies for the next spring's sledge journey, nearly a ton and a half in all, including every ounce of my alcohol and pemmican, were irrevocably and forever buried in the insatiate maw of the "Great Ice," and that all of the work of the past year had been completely blotted out. I was almost stunned by my loss; I felt like a man shipwrecked upon an uninhabited shore, with nothing left him but the clothes upon his back. . . .[17]

For the next few days Peary was deep in his depression, and his mood naturally set the tone in the Lodge. Henson was less affected than Lee, for he had his Eskimo friends to visit, he had Kudlooktoo to care for. He had learned from the Eskimos that laughter is the best antidote for the poison of failure, but neither Peary nor Lee was easily converted to this point of view. When Henson made small jokes they looked at him almost pityingly, as if he was not bright enough to understand the seriousness of their situation. Henson finally concluded that things would have to get worse before they got better. He was right.

Peary had given up the private room he had shared with his wife and now occupied the common room with his two subordinates. This sort of democracy in living was difficult for him; he was by nature a loner and did not take easily to the forced fraternity of bed, kitchen, and bath. But he was also a man of duty, and he performed one-third of the household chores, uncomplainingly and efficiently. He expected the same attitude and performance from the other two men.

There came a Wednesday when it was Hugh Lee's turn to cook. Lee was at the stove, Peary was reading, Henson was repairing the thongs on a snowshoe. The room was silent except for the slight sizzling sound of the whale fat in which some venison was being cooked. Whale fat is a difficult substance, for if not handled most carefully it has the tendency to ignite and burn in a smoky black flame that ruins food and makes the skillet difficult to clean.

This was what now happened. The whale fat ignited and sent up a flame and a sulfurous cloud of smoke. Lee retreated a step, then looked at the burning pan with venomous eyes, advanced to grab it by the handle; then he flung it with all his strength across the room. It hit the bottom of the door, shattered the wood panel, and disappeared, smoking and hissing, into the snowbank beyond.

Again there was silence, but this one was pregnant with the

emotions intensified by intimacy and isolation and defeat. Lee stood looking at the stove, breathing hard. Peary had dropped his book, his face flushed. Only Henson moved. He continued methodically to lace the thongs on the snowshoe. While the silence held, the Arctic air rushed in through the shattered door.

The loss of self-control was something Peary found intolerable. He never allowed it to happen to himself, and he was determined it should not happen to any of his men. He opened his mouth to dress down Lee, but the boy looked so woebegone that he could not bring himself to speak. He picked up his book and went on reading.

Lee now moved across the room, opened the door, and retrieved the blackened skillet. Then he got hammer and nails and some wood from a packing box and repaired the door. At last he returned to the stove and made another start at cooking dinner. When it was finally served, it was eaten in silence. And the men went to bed in silence. And arose in it again the next morning.

Henson made efforts at conversation but no one would pick it up and carry it on. Lee was now in the slough of guilt and self-pity. He would have preferred to have the commander bawl him out and have it over with. This way, it was as if Peary didn't even consider him worthy of discipline. He had acted like a child, and now Peary was treating him like one. He was feeling the lash of the terrible weapon of silence. And there was no escape.

As for Peary, once having ignored the outburst, he knew no way of coming back to it. And he was incapable of producing small talk to bury it. He, too, had feelings of guilt; he now believed he had shirked his duty by ignoring the incident.

And so the moods deepened and proliferated.

The following day it was Henson's turn to cook. He stood before the stove thoughtfully, then, unobserved, tilted the skillet so that the walrus fat ignited. The flame and black smoke ballooned up and he stepped back with an exclamation that brought Peary's and Lee's eyes upon him. Then he grabbed the skillet by the handle and flung it across the room where, with precise accuracy, it shattered the new panel Lee had put in the door, and disappeared into the snowbank beyond.

There was a moment of silent amazement, then a giggle from Lee, an answering one from Henson, and then all three men were roaring with laughter. And after the laughter came talk, blessed communication.

Laughter was what Peary had needed, not only to surmount the estrangement with Lee, but to sharpen his mind and refresh his spirit to take the big problem before them. That night he talked about it with his men.

"We'll have to get back to first principles on rations," he said. "Tomorrow we'll take stock of the frozen venison and walrus meat and see how far it will go in place of the lost pemmican. We can substitute coal oil for the lost alcohol. I think we can pull together rations of tea, biscuits, oil, and raw meat for us and the dogs sufficient for two months on the trail. That is enough for the trip to and from Independence Bay under good conditions. If the conditions turn bad, we'll have to live off what we can find on the ice cap."

All of them knew that game on the ice cap was nonexistent. The only living creatures they would find on the ice cap would be themselves and their dogs.

April 1, 1895, was the target date for departure and as the winter waned and the period of constant daylight approached, the tempo of preparation increased. The Eskimo women were urged to complete the fur garments, and as each was finished it was hung outdoors in the forty-degree-below-zero weather to kill any body lice that had crept into the seams from the seamstresses.

Henson completed the sledges and gave them trial runs. During the march he was to drive the largest, a catamaran sledge and trailer which would carry a tent and all supplies for the return trip. The weight would be about 1,000 pounds and it would be pulled by thirteen dogs. Two smaller sledges were also outfitted:

the *Josephine* to be driven by Peary, and the *Long Serpent* to be driven by Lee.

Six Eskimos were to help the party get the sledges up the steep slopes to the moraine and onto the ice cap, and four of them were to go as far as the site of the big cache, 128 miles from the Lodge. It was hoped that the Eskimos' fear of Kokoyah would not force them to turn back before that cache, and it was prayerfully hoped that that cache could be found. Despite their failure to find the caches closer at hand, they were buoyed by hope that the big one would be sufficiently near the surface to be found and retrieved.

The day before the departure, excitement ran through the camp. Henson, Lee, and Peary scrubbed themselves in their last baths, shaved, cut their hair short, and Peary even cut off his famous mustache. They turned in for a few hours' sleep.

The morning of April 1 was clear and cold, good sledging weather. The men rose, put on their clean new clothes, ate breakfast, and then proceeded to batten down the Lodge. All the valuable papers were put in a tin, fire-resistant box and stored under Peary's bunk. Supplies that were not to be taken on the trail were brought indoors from the snow tunnels and stored in the common room. The doors were closed and nailed shut. The company now assembled.

The Eskimos stepped forward from their friends and families. There were Nooktah, Kardahsu, Annowkah, Soker, Nupsah, and Akpudisoahho. There was a total starting party of six sledges and sixty dogs.

Peary took a last look around, then nodded to Henson that he could start the march. A small boy was standing shyly nearby; it was Kudlooktoo. Henson went up to him and put out his big hand. The boy took it, in American fashion, and smiled bravely. He was to stay with Ahnalka's wife.

"*Aksunai* (good-by)," Henson said.

"*Aksunai*," the boy replied.

Then Henson turned away and the march began.

[XI]

Three days' march, with a few hours' sleep snatched between, brought the party up the face of the glacier, across the moraine, and finally onto the ice cap. They were in the wasteland, the frozen desert, the white prairie of excruciating light.

The sun revolved in the heavens without setting, sending down its brilliance to be reflected on the gleaming snow and ice, to be multiplied and intensified, to become shattering shards of light that danced in the pure, rarefied air. For a man to spend a day on this plain without protection for his eyes would mean blindness.

Henson, Lee, and Peary wore the heaviest smoked sunglasses. The Eskimos wore their own protection—wooden eyecups with a tiny slit cut in the middle of them. When sleeping, all of them wrapped a band of fur across their eyes to keep the light from penetrating even through closed lids.

They pushed on into this inferno of whiteness, and at the end of the seventh march came to the site of the big cache, the place where Peary had been forced to turn back the year before, the place where he had deposited 1,400 pounds of pemmican. But there was no sign of it. A painstaking search was carried out for twenty-four hours by the entire party, but with no success. Failure to find the other caches had prepared them for this failure, to

A moment of relaxation aboard the *Windward* in New York harbor as Peary and Henson prepare for the abortive 1898 attempt on the Pole.

The Pole was won! And the ordeal was to be forever marked on his face.

Dr. Frederick A. Cook—ex-Peary assistant,
who claimed to have beaten Peary and Henson
to the Pole.

Robert E. Peary
poses in his furs.
(Bettmann Archive)

(Underwood & Und

The expedition ship *Roosevelt* dries her sails at Cape
Sheridan during the final and successful expedition north.

(Underwood & Underwood)

Searching the horizon from the top of the world
where every direction is south.

The climax of a life! Flanked
by his four Eskimo comrades,
Henson stands before the
American flag planted at the
North Pole on April 7, 1909.

(Underwood & Underwood)

Peter Freuchen, noted Danish explorer and correspondent, welcomes Henson to membership in the Explorers Club.

At last—the White House! President Dwight
Eisenhower receives Matthew and Lucy Henson on
April 6, 1954, the anniversary of the discovery
of the Pole.

MATTHEW ALEXANDER HENSON
CO-DISCOVERER OF THE NORTH POLE
WITH
ADMIRAL ROBERT EDWIN PEARY
APRIL 6, 1909
★ ★ ★ ★ ★ ★

BORN: AUGUST 8, 1866   DIED: MARCH 9, 1955

SON OF MARYLAND
EXEMPLIFICATION OF COURAGE, FORTITUDE AND PATRIOTISM,
WHOSE VALIANT DEEDS OF NOBLE DEVOTION
UNDER THE COMMAND OF ADMIRAL ROBERT EDWIN PEARY,
IN PIONEER ARCTIC EXPLORATION AND DISCOVERY,
ESTABLISHED EVERLASTING PRESTIGE AND GLORY
FOR HIS STATE AND COUNTRY

BY THE STATE OF MARYLAND
J. MILLARD TAWES, GOVERNOR
THE BOARD OF PUBLIC WORKS

J. MILLARD TAWES	GOVERNOR
LOUIS L. GOLDSTEIN	COMPTROLLER
HOOPER S. MILES	TREASURER
ANDREW HRUBECK, JR.	SECRETARY

THE GOVERNOR'S ADVISORY COMMITTEE

HERBERT M. FRISBY, CHAIRMAN	MRS. J. WILLIAM MIDDENDORF, JR.
SENATOR J. ALVIN JONES	ALBERT P. BACKHAUS

a degree, but they still hoped against hope that the big one would be found.

Peary took Henson aside for a sober discussion of the problem. "Matt, I really believed we'd find this one."

"I can take the Eskimos for another search after they've had a little rest."

Peary shook his head. "We've covered every inch of the area. The cache is down, down! We'll never find it, and we could never dig it out if we did find the marker. No, Matt, we've got to take a new look at our plans. This means that we go the rest of the way on frozen venison for us and frozen walrus meat for the dogs. We're a quarter way there; it's another four hundred miles to Independence Bay. Then if we find game we can cut north toward the Pole; if we don't we'll have to come five hundred miles back on what venison and walrus we have left on the sledges. It may not be enough."

"What if it runs out?" Henson asked, more to himself than to Peary.

Peary said quietly, "Then we eat the dogs." Both men thought a moment, then Peary said, "We can turn back now, Matt. What do you say?"

"What do you think the chances are, Commander?"

"I think we can make it."

"All right, sir, I think so, too. Let's push on."

"I'll speak to Lee and see how he feels."

"The Eskimos won't go any farther."

Peary clapped Henson on the shoulder and grinned. "You did a good job getting them this far."

Lee, too, wanted to go forward and so Henson went to say good-by to his Eskimo friends. They were squatted in a circle and their faces were worried, for they had guessed his decision.

Nooktah looked up and said, "Miy Paluk, you should come back with us."

"No, I must go on with Pearyaksoah."

"Kokoyah will not like it. What do you think happened to the food we look for today? Kokoyah buried it because he does not want you in his land. If you go out there, he will eat you."

Matt shook his head. "I do not believe in Kokoyah. I will prove to you he doesn't exist. I will go out there and I will come back."

The circle of men murmured disbelief and looked sad. Nooktah said, "We do not understand why you go. Back there—" he pointed back toward the Lodge—"are seal and walrus and igloos and women and children and friends and good laughter. Why is it you go the other way? Why do you go out there where there is nothing?"

Here was a question that went to the core of the man. He didn't know how to answer it very well; he could only say, "I go to find out, Nooktah. You say there is nothing, but maybe you are wrong. I want to see what's there with my own eyes." He grinned at his circle of friends. "When I come back I'll tell you what I have seen."

The morning of April 8 the Eskimos turned back. Their sturdy figures became gradually smaller and smaller, and then disappeared over the horizon. The three Americans were alone on the ice cap. With them were forty-two dogs.

The three men had covered about fifteen miles when Lee became sick and they made camp. Peary gave him medicine and put him to bed, then went to help Henson feed and tether the dogs. The moment the walrus meat was unloaded from the sledge and the dogs saw it, they set up a savage howl and made a dash for it, many of them pulling their stakes. Of this first feeding time, Peary wrote:

The care of the forty-odd dogs then fell upon Matt and myself, and to keep a pack of forty ravenous Eskimo dogs in order during feeding time is something beyond the power of two men. We succeeded in tying them as usual in groups of five to eight, to stakes driven in the snow about the camp, and Henson had nearly completed chopping up the daily ration of frozen walrus meat, while I, with whip in hand, tried to keep the yelping brutes from breaking loose. But it was impossible to be everywhere at once, and, while busy quieting one group, another, with a sudden combined rush, and the superhuman strength which the sight of food inspires in a hungry

Eskimo dog, tore up the stakes to which they were fastened, and dashed for the pile of meat. There was an instantaneous savage cry from every other dog, and in an instant every stake was broken or pulled up, and a howling avalanche of dogs swept through the camp and fell upon the meat. Each group being still fastened together by their traces, anything about the camp less firm than primeval rocks, such as projecting points of sledges, odometer, trailers, thermometer support, and so on, came to sudden grief.

Whip and voice were equally unheeded, and Matt and myself were obliged to jump out from among the furious animals, to save our foot-gear from being torn to pieces by their savage snaps at the meat and each other. . . . Here, before us, were forty-two savage, powerful dogs, the flower of the king-dogs and trained bear-hunters of the trip, mad with the struggle for food and the attacks on each other, and inextricably tangled and bound together by their traces—Kilkenny cats multiplied twenty-fold.

Then came the straightening out of the snarl. The temperature was 25 degrees below zero, and a strong wind was sweeping through the camp, loaded with a stinging drift of snow. Silently we went to work, and at the end of five hours had the Gordian knots untied and every dog secured, except one. He, tangled up and rendered helpless by the twisting traces, had been bitten by the others till he had gone mad with rage and pain, and, with bloodshot eyes, frothing at the mouth, and clashing teeth, bit at everything he could reach, until I was obliged to quiet him with a bullet.[18]

On April 12, the day following the struggle with the dogs, the party set out again, covering twelve miles. Lee claimed to feel better, but the truth was entered in his diary: "I am feeling quite sick, but I am better off with Peary and Matt than going back to the Lodge alone, but I am an awful drag on them. One more dog killed . . ."[19]

As they got under way Lee rode Henson's sledge, his own attached behind and his dogs added to the traces. This meant that Matt had to handle over twenty dogs in one all but unmanageable team. Soon a more serious problem faced the crippled party—a storm arose. It came in degrees, each phase more awesome than the one before.

First, formless clouds moved over the sun, making the sky disappear. Men and dogs moved through a gray nothingness—no sun, no sky, no horizon, not even any snow. The gray light seemed to come equally from above and below, suspending them in a vacuum. There was nothing the eye could rest on but themselves. Feet and snowshoes were sharply outlined, but they seemed to tread on nothingness. The sledge runners glided on the same nothingness.

The wind was gentle at first, hardly more than a breeze. Soon it increased in strength and whipped up the fine snow on the surface. The white opacity rose about a foot and a half, blanking out the sight of snowshoes; it was as if the men had been suddenly, painlessly truncated and were walking on the stumps of their legs.

Peary called a halt, and as Matt rushed to tether the dogs while Peary and the sick Lee struggled to put up their tent, the wind rose and hurled coarser and coarser snow at them. In a matter of minutes it became a roaring, blinding, suffocating Niagara of snow, making it almost impossible to breathe. At last the men fell into the tent and huddled together while the storm attacked their poor shelter.

The tent was entirely inadequate. The storm didn't rip it, but the cold invaded it, and when, after a few hours' sleep, Henson woke up he had a stiff, wooden feeling in his left cheek. He knew at once it had been frosted and he clapped his hands to it to warm the flesh and bring back the circulation.

"Commander! Commander!" he called. "Wake up."

Peary came alert at once and saw Henson holding his cheek. "Frosted?"

"Yes, sir, but not badly. You all right?"

Peary flexed his extremities. "No frost. Wake Lee."

"Hugh . . . wake up. Hugh!" Henson called, shaking the body next to them.

Lee came slowly awake. "Time to start?"

"Soon. See how your hands and feet are. I frosted a cheek."

Lee moved his fingers, then his toes, then a wondering look

came over his face. "My big toe"—he pointed to his left foot—"it feels wooden."

Without another word Henson knelt down and pulled off his boot and his woolen socks. The big toe was as white as if it were a plaster cast. Henson rubbed it briskly, but no color returned.

Peary leaned over anxiously and said, "More than frosted, I'm afraid. Looks frozen."

"We'll get some circulation back," Henson said grimly. He knelt before the reclining Lee, raised his own sealskin coat and placed Lee's foot on his bare belly, then pulled the coat back down. They crouched in this position for almost an hour, from time to time reaching up under Matt's coat to massage the ice-cold foot and toe. At last some streaks of red appeared to penetrate through the marble flesh; the circulation was returning.

That toe was to give Lee trouble the rest of the trip, however, and contribute to his incapacity, to the hated position of being a semi-invalid, a burden on his comrades.

The storm raged throughout the rest of that day and the three of them remained huddled in the tent. None of them, not even Henson, knew how to make the Eskimo snow igloo that would have given them proper protection, even some comfort.

The dogs suffered greatly from the storm, and when it came time finally to hitch them up, two were found useless and had to be shot. Six more days of marches followed, the termination of each march being forced by the exhaustion of the dogs. On April 20 only eight miles were covered. The dogs were simply not getting enough food to be able to pull the heavy loads over long distances.

Peary now took a desperate gamble. Though the supply of walrus meat was nearly exhausted, he fed the dogs double rations. With refreshed dogs they made marches of fifteen and ten miles during the next two days. But again they were faced with reduced rations, not only for dogs but for men.

They were now at 7,500 feet elevation and approaching the long spine of Greenland that ran north and south. They ruthlessly discharged all equipment not absolutely necessary; they iced the runners of the sledges to reduce friction; they resorted to every possible device to get more mileage. The temperature fluctuated between ten and forty-five degrees below zero and the effect on the dogs at this altitude was marked. They were weak and panting and had little stamina. Nor did the men. Both Henson and Lee were now bleeding at the nose.

The entries in Lee's diary during this period were few and poignant:

Sunday, April 21. Our dog food is rapidly being devoured, and we are not making very rapid progress. . . . We have to make more or we won't have enough dog meat to finish the trip.

Wednesday, April 24. This morning we discarded a lot of things we have decided to get along without.

Thursday, April 25. . . . my toe pained me so I could not stand it. . . . I had frozen the big toe on my left foot . . . took a big dose of morphine. . . .

Friday, April 26. . . . Taking morphine all day long . . .[20]

The big event that took place on Friday, April 26, didn't get into Lee's diary. Henson had been breaking trail with his double team and double sledge, on which lay the sick Lee, and about two o'clock in the afternoon he heard Peary hail him from behind. He stopped the dogs and waited for Peary's team to catch up.

There was excitement in Peary's voice when he said, "Matt, what do you notice about the weather?"

Henson looked around at the featureless landscape. It was a pitiless white day with enough wind to stir the dusting of snow at their feet. Nothing seemed unusual.

"The wind!" Peary insisted. "What do you notice about the wind?"

Now Henson understood and he broke into a broad grin. "It's at our back instead of our face!"

"Right! The wind is suddenly westerly. That means we've crossed the backbone, the continental divide!"

Peary had learned on his previous ice-cap trips that the regularity of the winds was phenomenal. The direction was always radial from the center of Greenland outward, and perpendicular to the nearest strip of coast. It was so steady as to be like a sheet of water descending the slopes of the Great Ice from the central dome outward to the coasts. Thus, the direction of the nearest land can be determined by the direction of the wind. They had faced into the wind up until this day; now they had the wind at their backs, for the nearest land was ahead, not behind them.

After a moment of elation, understandably brief, they resumed the march. The improvement of the wind direction was more than offset by the fact that the wear and tear on the sledges had brought them to imminent collapse. Within an hour one of the runners of Henson's tent sledge broke off. Henson repaired it by using one of the runners from the trailer sledge, thus abandoning the trailer. This repair lasted but a few miles and again the runner broke, this time beyond repair. Now a pair of skis had to be sacrificed to furnish runners for the tent sledge.

When they made camp that evening, Henson staked out the dogs and began to unpack their food. He looked at what was left. It was sufficient for a single meal. "Commander," he said to Peary, "starting tomorrow we'll have to start feeding the dogs to each other."

The next few days saw the poorest of the dogs slaughtered and served up as food, thus reducing their number to seventeen. In the few days after that, the number of dogs was reduced to eleven, and of the eleven three could hardly walk, let alone pull the sledges. Now the men got into the traces with the dogs. And one of the men had little strength.

Crippled, plucky Lee entered in his diary: "Monday, May 6. Nose and cheeks frozen repeatedly and covered with thick scabs, hair long and unbrushed. I have not washed. . . . My eyes are bloodshot from sunglare on the snow, and I walk lame from the frozen toe. It gives me a deal of pain, but I must walk just the same, and let it hurt."[21]

Now all food for the outward part of the trip had been consumed. Their situation was desperate. Peary took a reading of the sun's position and found they were at latitude 81 degrees, 14 minutes, and 5 seconds. They had to be near Independence Bay. Ahead they thought they saw the coastal land, but it might well be a mirage. If there was land, there could be game. But the party as a whole was used up. Neither Lee nor the majority of the dogs could go another step. If there was food up ahead, they could not go to it; it would have to be brought to them.

As the three men sat beside their sledges, chewing on the raw, frozen venison, each thought his own thoughts: Lee measured his own physical reserve, determined not to flunk out; Peary thought darkly on his destiny; Henson, a less complicated man, thought on the practical aspects of survival.

"I can take a gun and scout ahead to see if that is land," Henson said.

Peary looked up, shook himself free of his brooding, and said, "No, if it is moraine it will be full of crevasses. Too dangerous for one man in a weakened condition. We'll make camp here and tomorrow the two of us will make a reconnaissance."

They slept briefly, then rose to prepare for the trip to the distant cloud bank that could mean land, or be a mirage. Henson said, "We should take the chopsie sledge, sir. It's the lightest and we'll have to pull it ourselves." Peary looked at him questioningly, and Henson said, "If that is land, and we get down to the moraine and *don't* find food, the dogs would be too weak to climb back up and we'd have to abandon them."

Peary nodded his agreement, and the two of them, after making Lee as comfortable as possible in the tent, put themselves in the animal traces and pulled the small sledge behind as they headed toward the promising cloud.

[XII]

Tied to the sledge, their minds and bodies functioning on the animal level of savage hunger, Peary and Henson made their way over the remaining yards of the ice cap and came to the sight of earth. The land was not lush—it consisted of the broken and rocky fragments of the earth's skeleton—but it was land and they pressed feverishly toward it, their bloodshot eyes searching for game.

They came first to a series of huge concentric crevasses, ranged like the benches in an amphitheater and running from the crest nearly to the foot of the ice slopes leading down to the moraine. At their feet was a series of ice mounds, two to three feet high, formed by the freezing of the air exhaled from the crevasses. These mounds were covered with a dusting of fine snow and the crevasses beneath were difficult to detect.

The two men staggered onto the mounds and suddenly one of them disappeared. The snow mound had given way beneath Peary's feet and without a sound he had plunged downward. The mouth of the crevasse was narrow, and his shoulders had caught against the sides and suspended him. Beneath his dangling feet was a long drop and at the bottom jagged rocks to impale whatever came plummeting down upon them.

Henson dropped on his stomach and inched forward until he

was within inches of Peary. Neither man spoke; the rasp of their labored breathing was the only sound. Henson had cut loose the rawhide trace that ran from his harness to the sledge, and now he slipped it under Peary's arms, fastened it, and began to crawl backward. The harness tightened around Henson's shoulders; the trace tightened around Peary's chest. There was not sufficient leverage to pull Peary out of the crevasse but enough to keep him from plunging downward if he slipped. At this impasse they lay still for several moments to gather strength. Then, at a signal from Henson, Peary began to work his way upward, and each inch gained was at the cost of the rawhide's cutting under his armpits as Henson crawled backward.

After fifteen agonizing minutes Peary was waist-high out of the crevasse and lying forward on the surrounding snow. He was saved unless there was a new breakthrough. There was none, and soon the two men were lying side by side, breathing heavily with exertion and the stimulation of fear.

Slowly they climbed to their feet, staggering forward. Within minutes Henson disappeared. The mouth of this crevasse was narrower and he sank only to his waist. The same procedure of rescue was followed and experience gave them greater efficiency, but no less fear. Among the dangers was that of a broken leg. Six hundred miles from Anniversary Lodge, starving, with one sledge and no dogs, a broken leg would be fatal.

Still, hunger made them fatalistic and they walked straight ahead without searching out or trying to avoid the snow-covered crevasses. At last they came to the moraine, a rubble of rocks.

"Rocks once more, thank God!" Henson exclaimed as he stepped off the ice.

A short time later, with their footgear cut to ribbons and their feet bruised and bleeding, they longed for the smoothness of the ice.

On the moraine they found the tracks of Arctic hare and old droppings from musk ox, but that was all. The game had been here, but when? A week ago, a month ago, six months ago? Exhausted and discouraged, they turned back toward camp. It was twenty-five miles away. When they finally staggered into camp they received a weak but welcoming wave from Lee, who lay in the tent, white-faced with illness. Two more of the dogs had died.

After a small ration of frozen deer meat, they dropped down to sleep. Through Henson's drugged mind ran the words of Nooktah, spoken just before they parted: "You go out there and Kokoyah will eat you." He couldn't help wondering if the Eskimos were right after all. Perhaps there *was* a devil named Kokoyah who wanted no man on his ice cap. And perhaps he was indeed eating the three men who defied him. Henson smiled to himself ironically and thought that Kokoyah was a slow eater, certainly. He almost wished he'd hurry it up a bit.

Four hours later they awoke, had a ration of deer meat, and then Peary reviewed their situation. The purpose of the trip, he said, was to determine if the ice cap ran northward to the Pole, and if so, to follow it as far as possible. Obviously, they would have to surrender the hope of reaching the Pole, but he was reluctant to turn back without discovering if the Greenland land mass did indeed run northward to the top of the world, or if it ended in some sea.

They had come this far, and only a few miles more might reveal the ice cap's secret. Were they to turn back now? Perhaps they should. They had enough rations to see them back, or almost back, to Anniversary Lodge. The dogs had no food and would die, of course, but there was a fighting chance they could walk the 600 miles on the deer meat left. But they would have to start at once, if they were to go.

"On the other hand," Peary said, "there is musk ox some place in the moraine around Independence Bay. We could stake everything on a final hunt. And it would be *everything*. For if we went on and then failed to find the musk ox, we could never get back to the Lodge." He paused, looked intently at his two comrades for a moment, then said quietly, "I'm not going to make the decision. I leave it up to you."

After a moment's pause Henson said, "Let's make the hunt."

Lee, sick as he was, gallantly seconded Henson.

Peary nodded, flushed with gratitude. To cover his emotion he stood up abruptly and said, "We will name this bit of ice and snow 'Camp Resolution.'" Then he went about the business of harnessing the dogs to the sledge. They started north again, this time irrevocably committed.

Of this decision Peary wrote: "I felt . . . that in that cool, deliberate moment we took the golden bowl of life in our hands, and that the bowl had suddenly grown very fragile."[22]

They approached land on a more northerly course, and when they came to the moraine the elevation was higher and gave them a good view of Independence Bay and the distant shore. Hardly had they arrived at this vantage point than a storm descended upon them, a Niagara of wind and snow poured over them in their poor shelter, and they were held prisoners for two days.

On May 15 the storm ended and, leaving Lee in camp, Henson and Peary took the dogs, the guns and ammunition, three days' half-rations, and set out on the hunt that would save or doom them.

Again they had to make the tortuous descent over the crevasses that had eroded the descending face of the glacier. They headed toward a shallow canyon where Peary and Astrup had killed musk ox in 1892, and after twelve hours of steady marching they came to it. There was not a sign of game. This was the valley where Peary had staked his hopes. The two of them made a reconnaissance of the valley, but there was nothing.

They could only conclude that the animals were migratory. There was no way of knowing where the musk ox might now be, or when they'd return this way.

At this point two of the undernourished dogs, completely played out from the descent from the ice cap and the march over the moraine, developed piblokto and died in convulsions. Their bodies were fed to the remaining dogs.

There was nothing to do but keep walking. There was no purpose in returning to camp, no purpose in sitting in the valley empty of game. The next valley might be empty, and the next and the next, but there was nothing to do but keep walking until it was no longer possible to walk.

In the midst of the walking Peary saw a snow-covered rock move. He blinked his bloodshot, watering eyes. The rock moved again. Then it took the form of an Arctic hare.

"Matt . . . Matt!" he called weakly. "A hare. For God's sake, shoot it."

Henson was an excellent shot; that was why Peary turned to him in this moment of crisis and hope. Henson brought his gun to his shoulder, and the barrel wavered uncontrollably. He dropped to the ground, rested the gun on his knees, but though the gun was steadier, now his eyes began to blur. He fired, and the hare looked up quizzically and jumped off a few steps. Henson ripped off his sunglasses, stared hard against the cruel glare of the sun and snow, and fired again. The hare leaped into the air and fell dead. They pulled it apart and ate it, red and raw.

Here was the first full meal they had had since the Eskimos had left them, thirty-five days before, the first meal containing the proper nourishment that could fit a man for a full day's work. As they finished the last of the rabbit, it began to snow and they lay down to sleep, unmindful of the drifts that built up around their bodies. Henson thought to himself that they had tricked Kokoyah. But maybe Kokoyah had tricked them? Had he given them a rabbit, given them strength to continue a hunt that would end in failure? Was he teasing them?

Henson didn't believe in Kokoyah, of course; it was just a game he played. It was a game that he couldn't seem to help playing. It was easier to fight against something than against nothing. Perhaps this was the wisdom in the Eskimo legend.

Peary and Henson had, indeed, outwitted Kokoyah, for the next day they found musk ox. First they came upon a track, but it was so indistinct that they didn't allow themselves to believe their eyes. Still, their hearts responded and they pushed on excitedly. Then they came upon droppings . . . fresh ones! The animals were nearby!

Breasting a ridge, they saw a cluster of small black spots in the next valley. Glasses revealed the spots to be a herd of musk ox beginning their midday siesta. The herd numbered twenty-two cows and calves lying down while an old bull promenaded slowly near them. Two other bulls dozed nearby. Henson immediately tethered all the dogs so they couldn't run and alert the herd.

The two men were trembling with excitement as they conferred.

"We can't shoot from here," Henson said. "They're too far away."

Peary nodded. "There's nothing to do but rush them. They may hold their ground or they may break."

"Or," added Henson, "they may charge us."

"They may," Peary said.

A charging herd of musk ox would mean certain death for the men. They could not hope to shoot all the animals before being overrun and trampled. But death pressed in from so many sides that this aspect of it didn't seem any more threatening than the others.

Taking a deep breath and gathering what strength they had left, they charged the herd. Henson fired as he ran, his prayer speeding with the bullets. A bull sank to his haunches. Peary fired from the hip. Another one sank slowly down, blood gushing from just behind the foreshoulder. A third dropped, shaking a shaggy head and bellowing in anger and pain. Now the herd broke and the two men ran in pursuit, guns blazing.

Suddenly a wounded cow turned and lowered her head, her sharp horns glistening in the sun. Peary was almost upon her and his gun was empty. As he fumbled to reload, she charged him.

"Matt!" he cried out.

The enormous head with the small red eyes was almost upon him when there was the crack of a rifle. She staggered, tried to come on to gore the defenseless enemy before her, but couldn't make it. As she toppled over, Peary rose slowly to his feet and turned to look gratefully at Matt.

"It was my last bullet," Henson said with a wry grin.

Back in his lonely camp, Hugh Lee kept up daily entries in his diary. On Saturday, May 18, he wrote:

This is the fourth day that Lt. Peary and Matt have been away. They will be pretty hungry unless they have found musk-oxen, for they took but three days' food. . . . It is getting quite cloudy, and I'm afraid we're going to have a storm . . . would like to have them back before it begins. They have no tent, and very little in the way of sleeping gear, and they may suffer a great deal if it storms. . . . Something may have happened to Lt. Peary and Matt that [would] make me a solitary sojourner in this desolate land, but I will try not to think of that yet.

Sunday, May 19. Last night, a little before midnight, I heard Matt's voice singing at the top of his lungs—the sweetest song I ever heard. I started the lamp, for I know hot tea would be in demand. Then I went to greet them.[23]

Musk oxen made it possible for Peary to carry out his geographical observations and he discovered that the Greenland ice cap was not at all the "imperial highway" to the North Pole. Running east from Independence Bay was water that appeared to terminate Greenland. . . . They were on an island, a gigantic island to be sure, but one that did not afford easy access to the North Pole. That was what Peary had come to find out.

Now the problem was to get three men back over the ice cap to Anniversary Lodge 600 miles away. They had a broken sledge, a few worn dogs, and an inadequate supply of food, including the heavy musk-ox meat.

It became a race with death that was won by the narrowest margin. One after another of the remaining dogs wore out and had to be destroyed. The men pulled the sledge themselves, and their condition became not much better than the dogs'. Lee had been suffering from constipation which had turned to diarrhea. His illness grew worse until he was unable to keep anything on his stomach. He became progressively weaker. On June 9 he was so weak he had to lie down to rest, and when he tried to get up, he was unable to do so and the other two men were nearly a mile ahead. He wrote:

It did not seem to me as though I could overtake them, as I could hardly drag one foot behind the other, and I lay down and watched them going farther and farther away from me, Peary in the lead, followed by the dogteam and Matt walking beside the sledge.

Finally Peary looked around and saw me lying on the snow. He halted the team and started to come back to me. I could not bear to think of him after he had covered that mile coming back to me and then having to retrace it again, so I staggered to my feet and motioned to him to stay where he was.

Eventually I got to them and dropped down on the snow. I told Peary to go on without me, as I was unable to travel and they could not carry me on the sledge. I told them delay would endanger their lives, so it would be foolish for them to stop. I told them goodbye and wished them good luck, telling them I was finished.

Peary said: "We will have no more of that kind of talk. We will all get home or none of us will. A rest would do us all good anyway, and we will camp here for a day and see what the situation is at the end of that time."[24]

They camped and Peary and Henson took turns nursing Lee, seeing that he didn't get more frostbite and that he hourly took cups of liquid with beef peptonoids and brandy in it. At the end of twenty-four hours he was able to stand and walk. The march was resumed.

They had a hundred more miles to go.

On the last camp, from where they could make out the summits of the Whale Sound mountains, they had the very last of their rations—a cup of tea with canned milk and four biscuits. One dog remained alive. Henson fed him a pair of sealskin boots and a few yards of rawhide line.

The next day they made Anniversary Lodge. Peary wrote:

"Even should I in the hereafter be permitted to gaze upon the glory of the Golden City, the sight of its splendour will not outburn the peerless view that met my blurred eyes as I rounded the last angle of the rocks and saw before me . . . Food. Rest. Heaven."[25]

It was June 25. They had been on the ice cap eighty-six days, walked 1,600 miles, been near death several times, but they had survived. Kokoyah had been disproved, or at least defeated. Now they lay in their bunks and slept, and awoke to eat, and slept again.

And awoke for longer, more clearheaded periods during which they thought on what had happened.

It became clear to Peary that young Lee's physical condition would not allow him to return to Arctic exploration, which was a pity because his temperament was right and his courage boundless. No, on future expeditions he would have to rely increasingly on Henson. He began to realize how inextricably they were really tied together.

It wasn't just that Henson had twice saved his life—there was no sentiment involved—but the sober realization that he had never had a man on the trail quite like Henson: strong, tenacious, skillful, and above all cheerful. It was not a mindless grinning, but a sort of happy fatalism. Henson was the true adventurer, a man eager to pit himself against the storm when the outcome could only be in doubt.

Peary and Henson complemented each other. Henson was the artisan, the dogteam driver, the carpenter, tinkerer, hunter. Peary was the intellectual, the dreamer and philosopher, the bold strategist. Both men were brave; both were gamblers in a game they could not leave, whatever the losses.

It was not easy for Peary to accept this new relationship. If it had been feasible he would have surrounded himself with fraternity brothers from Bowdoin College (he carried the Delta Kappa Epsilon fraternity flag with him on his expeditions). In the person of an uneducated Negro there had appeared the qualities he so desperately needed but had largely failed to find among the gentlemen.

Typical of Peary, once he had made a decision as to what was right and necessary, nothing could sway him. No amount of criticism, and there was to be much, could alter his determination to have Henson at his side. Henceforth, in his writings he praised Henson highly and referred to him as "my faithful colored assistant." He couldn't bring himself to drop the word "colored," but he steadfastly and courageously clung to the word "assistant."

[XIII]

The relief ship *Kite* appeared on schedule, and Henson nailed shut all the windows and doors of Anniversary Lodge. He said good-by to his Eskimo friends and to Kudlooktoo, assuring them he would return, if not to this Lodge, at least to Greenland, to the North. Though Peary had spoken of no future plans, he knew the man.

On the return trip Peary insisted on stopping in Melville Bay to take aboard two of the saviksue (meteorites) he had previously located. Returning defeated in his effort toward the Pole, he wanted at least to deliver these important minerological specimens to America.

They were almost back to New York before he said to Henson, quite casually, "The next trip will have to be longer. We need to establish a base and then work out of it for at least four years. With sufficient gear and supplies we are certain to make the Pole in that period. I'll start raising funds the minute we get home."

Henson grinned. "That's one department I can't help much in."

"You'll come back north with me, Matt?"

"Yes, sir."

"I don't know how long it will be before I can get the backing for the next expedition. I'll try and find you a job in the mean-time."

"Don't worry about me. I'll find something."

When the *Kite* arrived in New York harbor the returning explorers were greeted, if not as conquering heroes, at least as brave men who had spent time in a fascinating wilderness. Crowds came aboard to look at the equipment and trophies, but none was more eager and excited than a plump little man who was a curator of the Museum of Natural History. He had commissioned Peary to bring back northern flora and fauna and artifacts. He looked over the hides of musk ox and walrus and hare, rubbing his hands in pleasure.

"Excellent specimens," he said, beaming on Peary. "Excellent . . . excellent. And such a deft job of skinning. All too often the skins are butchered, but you, sir, did a magnificent job."

"I didn't do them," Peary said. "My assistant, Matt Henson, did the skinning."

The curator looked at Matt in surprise. "You did this work?"

"Yes, sir."

"Have you ever done taxidermy?"

"No, but if I can skin animals I imagine I could stuff them. Why?"

"It occurs to me that you can be of great assistance in mounting these specimens. We plan an Arctic exhibit, with the native wild life mounted realistically before painted backgrounds. If you'd like to give us a hand, I'll be happy to give you a job."

"I'll take the job," Henson said with a grin.

In the spring of 1896 Henson took a leave of absence from the museum to go north with Peary to bring back the big Agnighito meteorite, and when this ended in failure, went north with him on the same mission in 1897, which was a success.

His work at the museum was interesting, and it served the important purpose of killing time and supplying food and shelter until the next assault on the Pole. But also, it plunged him back into the old problem of Negro-white relations. One of the friends he made was a Negro named George Gardner. Gardner was an intelligent and race-conscious man and greatly admired Henson. One evening at his apartment he burst out, "Matt, I'm so glad you're going to stick with Peary. It's important you do this for our race."

"Our race?" Matt repeated, confused.

"Of course, of course! Don't you see what a tribute it would be to all Negroes if you are able to get to the Pole? Think, man, what it means to a minority to have one of its members a national hero!"

"I hadn't thought much about that," Henson said.

"You haven't thought about the race problem?" Gardner demanded, aghast.

Henson was embarrassed. "Yes, in a way, of course. But you see—" he grinned apologetically—"in the North us Eskimos are in the majority. I guess when you're in the majority you just don't think much about the problem."

Peary had little trouble raising the money for the next expedition, or for the series of them that followed over the next eleven years. By this time he had become a national hero and his determination to "capture the Pole for America" was a patriotic project in which millions of men and women vicariously participated. Here was adventure and heroism and competition with foreigners, all the elements necessary to call forth a great emotional outpouring.

Just as in the mid-twentieth century the probing of space by the astronauts was to bring thrills and pride to every American, so at the turn of the century the invasion of the Arctic was avidly followed by an entire nation. And in Peary's time the Arctic seemed as remote and mysterious and beckoning as does outer space today. If John Glenn or some other astronaut were to bring back a man from Mars, the astonishment would be some greater, but not much, than when Peary and Henson brought back the first Eskimos.

On January 12, 1897, Peary was awarded the Cullom Gold Medal of the American Geographical Society. He traveled to England to receive the Royal Geographical Society's Patron's Gold

Medal. He was given numberless testimonial dinners and banquets, and in 1898 twenty-five prominent and wealthy Americans formed the Peary Arctic Club and promised to underwrite the costs involved in his assaults on the Pole.

In 1898, when he again prepared to sail north, Peary was the subject of an outpouring of poetry. Elsa Barker, in a poem entitled "The Frozen Grail," wrote:

> What shall prevail against the spirit of man,
> When cold, the lean and snarling wolf of hunger,
> The threatening spear of ice-mailed Solitude,
> Silence and space and ghostly-footed Fear
> Prevail not? Dante in his frozen hell,
> Shivering, endured no bleakness like the void
> These men have warmed with their own flaming will,
> And peopled with their dreams.

Richard Le Gallienne wrote:

> Peary, Godspeed!
> I hardly know
> The vast and intricate significance
> Of all that snow
> To which you go;
> I only understand
> A brave man dares again.
> When heroes fight
> Who asks his trivial why
> So that they fight like heroes.

There were no medals struck off for Henson, of course, and no poems written about him. The few occasions his name did appear in the press it was linked to the stereotyped "Peary's Negro servant." But the men who backed the expedition knew his worth, and when the list of personnel in the new expedition was published, it gave Matthew Henson as "assistant."

This time Peary planned a sustained assault on the Pole. He had sufficient funds and supplies so that if he didn't win his objective the first year, he would stay in the North and try for the prize the second year. If that failed, he would try the third year, and again the fourth. He would sail a ship right up through the ice-choked Kane Basin and Kennedy Channel to establish a base on the very shore of what he called the "Polar Sea." Then he had but to march over the ice cap to the Pole and back. He could not conceive of failing four times in a row.

Peary's "Polar Sea" was actually that part of the Atlantic Ocean north of the land masses of Greenland and Ellesmere Island. As opposed to the Antarctic, which is land, the Arctic is a variety of oceans and seas on which floats a massive and permanent ice cap. When Peary spoke of entering upon the Polar Sea, or the Arctic Sea, he meant he was advancing over this ice cap toward the Pole.

In the midsummer of 1898 Peary and Henson sailed north to Etah, an Eskimo settlement on the coast of Greenland north of the old headquarters of both Red Cliff House and Anniversary Lodge. There they had a reunion with their old friends, took them and their dogs on board, and headed north into the Kane Basin. But on August 18 their ship, the *Windward*, was caught in a gigantic ice floe and imprisoned throughout the winter.

This meant that the expedition would now have to trek supplies 400 miles over the ice to reach a base on the shore of the Polar Sea to which Peary had hoped to sail! Peary and Henson resolutely faced up to the job and began moving supplies, Eskimos, and dogs to the western shore of the Kane Basin, establishing a temporary base at Cape D'Urville on Ellesmere Island.

The long Arctic winter had now settled over the expedition but it would be possible to sledge supplies northward during the period of the moons. Consulting his charts one night, Peary said to Henson, "Matt, we can make it to the Polar Sea in two stages instead of one. About two hundred fifty miles north of here is Fort Conger, Greely's old base."

"Would his buildings still be standing?" Matt asked.

"No one knows, but they might be. As soon as the December moon arrives, we'll start sledging to Fort Conger. By double-banking we should be able to get all our equipment there by spring;

then we'll be in a much better position to strike for the ice cap."

This was a fateful decision. Not only was the journey to be made in terrible cold and partly in darkness, not only did it come near to ending Peary's career, but the selection of Fort Conger as a base was to result in Peary's writing words about the Greely expedition that would, eleven years later, bear bitter fruit during the Cook controversy.

Back in the summer of 1881, as part of the International Polar Year, the United States had sent north an expedition under the direction of the Army and commanded by Major Adolphus W. Greely. It was an expedition of unrelieved tragedy, marked by executions and death by starvation. The major, two lieutenants, one doctor, ten sergeants, one corporal, and nine privates were put ashore at Discovery Harbor, high up on Ellesmere Island, and were promised a relief ship the following year. That ship couldn't make it through the ice. A second relief ship was sent north but that, too, failed to penetrate the Kane Basin.

In the fall of 1883 Greely broke camp at Fort Conger and began to march southward, hoping to meet any ship that might be trying to reach him. The men froze, starved, were lost, died one by one. When the rescue partly finally reached them, Greely was the only commissioned officer left and there were only six other pathetic survivors barely alive.

When Peary made his decision to march for Fort Conger, Greely was back home, a General in the Army and a hero to the nation. And he was a proud and jealous man. He was to become furious over Peary's criticism of his expedition.

On December 29 Peary and Henson, with light sledges and four Eskimos, started north. On midnight of January 6 they came upon the dilapidated, snowdrifted, but still erect and tar-paper-covered buildings of Fort Conger. Henson started the stove in the officers' quarters and then lighted the range in the kitchen. By the light of the fires they looked around the fateful quarters.

The place was littered with a heartbreaking array of personal belongings: photographs of wives and children, diaries, good-luck charms, bits of clothing, all left behind to testify to the tragedy that had stalked these men sixteen years ago.

As they inspected the quarters Peary suddenly stood quite still, his head slightly to one side as if listening for a distant sound.

"Matt . . ."

"Yes, Lieutenant?"

"There's a wooden feeling in my feet."

Matt looked quickly at him, then tried to match the calm tones just spoken. "Sit down and let me take off your kamiks." Off came the boots, and then the soft skin socks beneath, and finally the wool beneath that. Both feet were marble-white, badly frosted. At once Matt fell to his knees in front of Peary, pulled up his own clothes, and put the iced feet against the warm, dark skin of his belly. He held them there for an hour, from time to time rubbing the feet with his hands. Slowly the color came back to the blanched feet, and with it came the awakening of the nerves, causing Peary to clamp his teeth together. But the toes did not resume their natural pinkness; they turned blue-black as the blood went into the lifeless tissue.

Henson bathed the feet in a solution of iodine crystals found in Greely's medicine chest, then ordered Ahnidloo and Sipsoo, two of the Eskimos who squatted glumly on the floor, to make up a cot with fur robes. He lifted Peary in his arms and carried him to the cot.

From January 6 to February 18 Peary lay on his back in the dreary camp while Henson nursed him. He was racked with pain from his frozen feet, but the mental anguish was far greater. If he lost his toes his entire balance on snowshoes would be affected. Without snowshoes a man couldn't get to the North Pole. After trying and suffering for so many years, was he to be defeated in this bleak camp of death willed him by Greely? He brought to bear upon himself all the force of will and determination he could gather.

In the midst of his agony he grabbed up a pencil and wrote on the wall above his coat, "*Viam invenian aut faciam.*" Then he threw the pencil across the room. During the next day Henson looked at the strange words several times, then finally asked what they meant.

Peary explained they were first written by the Latin philosopher Annaeus Seneca who was born in 4 B.C. The words? "I shall find a way or make one."

At the end of six weeks Peary still could not stand, the toes were still black, there would be no miracle of recovery, Seneca or not. He faced this fact as he faced all defeats, with a cold and angry briskness. He said, "Matt, I've got to get back to the ship and have the doctor cut off these toes. Can you get me there?"

"Yes, sir, I can," Matt said.

Henson lashed Peary firmly to a sledge and set out from Fort Conger for the *Windward*, 250 miles away. The ice was a rubble of vicious peaks and crevasses and the temperature averaged fifty-six degrees below zero. The sledge slid and toppled, but Henson pushed and heaved and cried at the dogs and Eskimos and forced them onward. In eleven marches, averaging 22.75 miles, they made the ship.

On March 13 the doctor operated on Peary, removing all but the little toe on each foot. A man without toes would find it difficult to keep his balance on a city street; to do so in the Arctic would seem impossible.

[XIV]

News of Peary's condition was sent back to the New York members of the Peary Arctic Club and all of them assumed this to be the end of the expedition. They were wrong. Within an incredibly short time after the operation Peary and Henson were again sledging supplies northward to the advance base at Fort Conger. If Henson hadn't been strong enough to handle a sledge on which the invalid Peary was lashed, or skillful enough to handle the dog-team, the trips could not have been made. If Peary had not had the iron will, the trips could not have been made. Here, as in previous crises, the two men's divergent talents and skills combined to form the necessary whole.

Fort Conger was reached on April 28; the return trip to the ship was completed on July 28. The first year of the four-year expedition was drawing to a close without their ever having been out on the Polar ice cap. Still, they had established a continuous line of depots between the ship and Fort Conger, and they had established the fact that musk oxen abounded in the Conger area.

On August 2 the *Windward* was finally released from the ice and immediately got up steam to escape southward before being caught for another winter. Peary and Henson were left behind in

Etah, Greenland, where they spent the winter living with the Eskimos. During that winter Henson and his Eskimo friends sledged additional supplies across the frozen waters of Kane Basin to the western shore and northward to Fort Conger.

The spring assault on the Pole was undertaken by Peary in March. He joined Henson at Fort Conger on March 28, 1900, noting in his journal: "The process of breaking in the tendons and muscles of my feet to their new relations and the callousing of the amputation scars has been disagreeable."[26]

That was, no doubt, an understatement.

On April 9 seven sledges turned eastward across the Kennedy Channel and headed toward the northern coast of Greenland which was to be the jumping-off point for the ice cap. The Eskimos began to weaken in their will as they got near the frozen sea; they had never been on it and believed it was the abode of evil spirits. Soon there were only Peary, Henson, and the Eskimo Ahmmahlakoto left in the party, and the dogs began to die at an unprecedented rate. Circumstances were again combining to baffle and frustrate Peary and Henson.

At last they reached the most northern part of land in the world, the tip of Greenland, which Peary named after one of his financial backers, Cape Morris K. Jesup.

The ice northward, out on the sea, was in a frightful condition, jammed and broken into mountainous ridges. The party had the strength to travel onto it but a little way. They reached the latitude of 83 degrees, 50 minutes north. Then they turned back.

The second attempt of the projected four had failed.

When they returned to Fort Conger on June 10, the summer thaw had set in and opened stretches of water, preventing them from going back south and east to Etah. In consultation, Peary and Henson decided to stay through the winter at Fort Conger and try to live off the land. Henson's skill with the rifle and the prevalence of musk ox saved them from starvation that winter.

On April 5, 1901 the third attempt was launched. Peary, Henson, one Eskimo, two sledges, and twelve dogs started north. This attempt was brave to the point of foolhardiness. Neither men nor animals were in condition to win this gamble. Supplies and equipment were inadequate; morale was low. At Lincoln Bay, with the Polar ice cap beckoning just beyond, the strength of all failed simultaneously and they turned back.

The Peary Arctic Club sent the *Windward* north again that spring with fresh supplies for the stubborn pair, and followed her up with the *Erik*. Now there was an abundance of equipment and food, but as the early spring of 1902 approached, a new problem arose—the Eskimos began to balk at going north again.

They were at Fort Conger, it was March 23, and the drive to the Pole was to start the following day. Suddenly the Eskimos sat down sullenly beside their sledges, refusing to pack them. "What is it?" Peary demanded of Henson. "What's gotten into them?"

"It's that damned devil of theirs," Henson said. "The frozen sea is supposed to be the home of the special devil, a character named Tahnusuk. And they don't want to visit him."

"Send them to me," Peary snapped.

The Eskimos filed into the common room and stood dutifully before their commander. They were a little shamefaced, and Peary started out with a fatherly tone:

"This year there is plenty of food for you and your dogs. When we return I will give you rifles and bullets and knives so you can be great hunters and always be sure of plenty of food for your families."

One of the Eskimos said, "That is no use to us if Tahnusuk does not let us come back, if Tahnusuk eat us up."

"There is no Tahnusuk!" Peary burst out. "Can't you understand that? There just isn't any Tahnusuk!"

The Eskimos stood in silence, unmoved. Centuries of native lore was not going to be banished by a mere statement from a kabloona. Peary paced the room, angrily searching for the key to these people. He swung around to face them, crying again, "It is all in your imagination. There is no devil out there waiting to eat you. Believe me!"

One of the Eskimos stepped forward and said, "You should know the power of Tahnusuk. Three times he has warned you away from his home. When you first start, he freezes your feet. Then you go again and he nearly starves you and Miy Paluk and Ahmmahlakto and he brings great storms to kill the dogs. Then you go again and you are caught by open water and ice that is thrown high into the sky. Who do you think could do such things to you but Tahnusuk? Now, if you go again, he will not be so kind. This time he will eat you . . . and everyone who goes with you."

After this declaration there seemed nothing more to be said, so the Eskimos filed out of the room, leaving Peary and Henson facing each other. After a moment of silence Peary said, "Matt, go talk to them."

"Yes, sir," Matt said, but his tone was dubious.

"If you can't get them to change their minds, we'll go north alone."

"The two of us couldn't make it alone. We just couldn't sledge enough supplies."

Peary said coldly, "The two of us will go. Or, if necessary, I'll go alone."

"It will be the two of us," Henson said.

Henson went out to talk to the Eskimos and was gone for about fifteen minutes. When he came back there was a grin on his face. "It's okay," he announced. Peary looked out to see that the Eskimos were indeed packing the sledges. As a good commander, he did not question Henson on what means he had used to carry out orders. It was sufficient that he had done so.

On March 24 they all left Fort Conger for the Pole.

It was not until two days later that Peary brought up the question. He said, "Matt, how did you get the Eskimos to come with us?"

Henson grinned. "I told them you were a greater devil than Tahnusuk."

"What?" Peary exclaimed.

"Well, in a way, I did. I told them that in the South was the most powerful devil in all the seas, the United States Navy. And since you were a member of the Navy, you were more than a match for Tahnusuk. I said you could defeat him every time."

With a wry smile Peary said, "Let's hope you're right."

From Fort Conger they marched to Cape Hecla and there swung straight northward over the Polar ice cap. The little caravan had been in the field a month, had traveled over 400 miles in temperatures down to sixty degrees below zero, yet the main struggle was before them. It was another 400 miles to the Pole and, of course, the same distance back.

All through April the four Eskimos followed Henson and Peary, but with increasing apprehension. To conserve food Peary sent two Eskimos back to shore, leaving a total of four men and three sledges and teams. Finally, the two remaining Eskimos gave up, licked by both exhaustion and fear of Tahnusuk. Many of the dogs had died; those still on their feet were in poor condition. The end of the trail had been reached.

On April 21, 1902, Peary entered these somber words in his journal: "The game is off. My dream of sixteen years is ended. It cleared during the night and we got under way this morning. Deep snow. Two small old floes. Then came another region of old rubble and deep snow. A survey from the top of a pinnacle showed this extending north, east and west, as far as could be seen. The two old floes, over which we had just come, are the only ones in sight. It is impracticable, and I gave the order to camp. I have made the best fight I know. I believe it has been a good one. I cannot accomplish the impossible."[27]

The return home was full of suffering, but Peary's mental anguish over failure inured him to the pains in his body. There were several hairbreadth escapes which he hardly noticed; he seemed unconcerned with the fate of a body and a will that had failed him. The dogs died, food gave out, the Eskimos panicked; it was Henson who kept the caravan together and headed south. After a summer full of incredible misery they saw the *Windward* heave into sight on August 5.

Peary's wife and daughter had come north on the *Windward*, and they lifted his spirits somewhat. As he paced the deck of the ship, walking unsteadily on his butchered feet, he began to find some compensation for the four years of struggle and pain. On this final try he had reached 84 degrees, 17 minutes north latitude. The Pole, at 90 degrees, was still 343 nautical miles distant, but he had made a record. He'd gone farther north than any other living man. If he hadn't won his entire fight, he had retreated honorably and with a degree of victory.

Then they broke the shattering news to him. While he and Henson had been in the North these last four years, the Duke of Abruzzi, brother of King Humbert of Italy, had organized an expedition that had reached 86 degrees, 34 minutes north latitude. He had beaten Peary by over twenty miles.

This news acted differently on Peary than it would on many men. This was the sort of wormwood he needed to shake off the self-pity that had enveloped him. He could accept defeat by nature, but never at the hands of another man. He saw the Duke and his record as deadly and personal enemies who had to be vanquished, no matter what the cost.

As the *Windward* got under way for New York, Henson stopped by Peary's cabin to find him poring over his old charts of the coasts of Greenland and Ellesmere Island. "We've got to get a boat right into the edge of the Polar Sea, Matt. Our base has always been too far south. A boat has got to ram its way through Kennedy and Robeson Channels and right into the Polar Sea!"

Amazed at both his new cheerfulness and the audacity of his thinking, Henson exclaimed, "Why, there's no boat built that could do that."

Peary grinned and said, "Quite right, Matt. We're just going to have to build one."

[XV]

When Peary and Henson returned home they found Teddy Roosevelt in the White House and the country in the mood for heroic events. The two explorers were cheered and feted, their failure to reach the Pole forgotten in admiration for their gallant effort. The President was preaching America's destiny through the strenuous life, and what two better examples of his philosophy in action than these assaults on the mysterious North?

Henson and Peary were heroes on widely separate levels of society, of course. Peary would not have been so warmly received in Henson's world, and Henson not at all in Peary's. From the equality of the northern wilderness they had returned to civilization where their skin colors set them apart. They might sleep together in an igloo, but could not sit together at the same banquet table in a New York hotel.

Peary's honors came rapidly that fall and winter. He was invited to address the Royal Geographical Society; was given a testimonial dinner by the University Club of New York; received the Royal Scottish Geographical Society's coveted Livingston Gold Medal; received the gold medal of the *Société de Géographie* of Paris; was elected President of the American Geographical Society; was advanced by the Navy (despite the jealousy of the line officers) from Lieutenant to Commander in the Civil Engineers' Corps.

Henson, on the other hand, disappeared into that subterranean world of the Negroes. He was not to emerge again until Peary was ready for the next assault on the Pole. For a time he relaxed in New York, visiting with friends he had made while at the Museum of Natural History, telling stories of the North to small groups in Harlem, and paying particular attention to a young lady by the name of Lucy Ross.

He first met Lucy at George Gardner's apartment. The host had invited a number of leading Negroes for dinner, not only to hear Henson's stories but, in this small way, to honor him. Lucy was hardly a leader in Harlem; she was the daughter of a widowed neighbor and Gardner had invited them as an act of kindness. But when Lucy entered the room, Matt Henson directed all his remarks to her.

She was young and bright and interested. She had a job as a clerk in a large bank, one of the first Negro girls to break through the racial barriers in the banking system, and she wasn't intimidated by this big explorer—she was simply fascinated.

"Are the Eskimo women pretty?" Lucy asked demurely, with womanly wisdom.

Henson, who at thirty-five seemed a confirmed bachelor, did not know how to play the game. "Yes, they are pretty," he said. Then, seeing the look of disappointment on the girl's face, he hastily added, "At least, the Eskimo men think they're pretty."

Everyone laughed except Mrs. Ross, Lucy's mother. She said, "Isn't it true they're very dirty?"

"Well," said Matt, "I suppose so. They don't have bathtubs or running water, so it's difficult for them to keep clean. They clean themselves by rubbing the greasy dirt from their bodies with a birdskin, then they hang the skin outdoors to dry and freeze, then beat off the frozen dirt with a seal bone. If we lived where they do, we'd have to bathe in the same way."

Mrs. Ross wasn't satisfied. She snapped, "They're supposed to be very immoral. Isn't that true?"

Dr. Frederick Cook had been lecturing around the country ever since his trip north with Henson and Peary, and some of his more lurid details of Eskimo life had been fully reported in the press. Mrs. Ross was obviously a reader of the Cook stories.

Immoral? Henson had to reorient himself. They hadn't seemed so to him in the North, but, of course, there were different standards back here in civilization.

"They don't get married!" Mrs. Ross cried, triumphantly.

"No, not in a church," Henson admitted. "They don't have any churches. But when a man takes a woman he considers her his wife and he cares for her, feeds her, hunts animals to clothe her. They never lie to each other; they never desert each other. In some ways they are more moral than we are."

"But . . . ," trumpeted Mrs. Ross.

Matt held up his hand. "I know what you're going to say. They sometimes trade around their wives. And it's true. But nobody gets hurt feelings, or thinks they are unwanted; it's the custom. And if a woman has a baby by another man, the husband takes her back and the baby, too. All the children are loved . . . by everyone. I know it's wrong by our code, but not by theirs. And all I can say is that the Eskimo families are happier than most of the families back here."

There followed a lively discussion about the moralities involved, and if Mrs. Ross carried the day, it was because she was the loudest and, of course, had the backing of all women present. Lucy Ross did not take part in the argument, but her eyes revealed that she thought Matt Henson pretty wonderful even if he did say outrageous things.

It was with some emotional pain that later in the week Matt informed Lucy he had to leave New York. He had gotten a job as a Pullman porter on a line running west out of Chicago.

While Henson was making up sleeper beds, Peary took to a hospital bed in Philadelphia. With typical thoroughness, he was preparing himself for the next trip north and had instructed Dr. W. W. Keen to repair his feet so that he might walk better. His two remaining little toes projected beyond the stumps of the others, making an uneven and tender area. Dr. Keen amputated the outer joint of each little toe to bring them in line with the stumps. Then, slitting the skin at the front of the feet, the tissue from beneath and behind the toes was drawn forward to make a cushion for the stumps and ease the pain of marching.

Once out of the hospital, Peary devoted all his energies to raising funds to build a ship that would be capable of smashing its way to the Arctic Sea. This was accomplished, and on October 15, 1904 the keel was laid. The ship was to be built to his own specifications.

This ship was to be a steam vessel with auxiliary sails which could be used to save fuel in the Far North. Her proportions were of a Scotch whaler, stubby and maneuverable. Her over-all length was 184 feet, with a beam of 35½ feet, and a draft load of 16 feet. The shallow draft was to permit her to get inshore and around icebergs.

The wooden sides of the ship were massive in thickness and heavily braced. Her outer shell was steel-sheathed. Her counter was raked to protect the propeller and rudder, and her bow raked to allow her to ride over the ice floes when she rammed them. The quarters for crew and expedition members were on deck with the great holds below reserved for coal. Also on deck were powerful appliances—windlass, steam capstan, and winch—which could warp the vessel out of dangerous positions near shore and in the ice packs.

The ship was launched on March 23, 1905. Mrs. Peary shattered a block of ice, which contained a bottle of champagne, against the stern, and the ship was named *Roosevelt*.

Peary wrote: "When it came to finding a name for the ship by whose aid I hoped to fight my way toward the most inaccessible spot on earth, the name *Roosevelt* seemed to me to be the one inevitable name. It held up as an ideal before the expedition those very qualities of strength, insistence, persistence, and unvarying victory over all obstacles, which made the twenty-sixth President of the United States so great."[28]

The *Roosevelt* sailed north out of New York harbor on July 16,

1905. It was Henson's sixth expedition north. When Henson came aboard he found that the crew and the expedition members were all greenhorns as far as the frozen sea was concerned. But then, all mankind, with the exception of Peary, Henson, and four Eskimos, were greenhorns in that remote area. Still, it seemed to Henson that for each expedition he had to start all over to teach the way of northern life: how to dress and eat and sleep in order to survive. He was impressed by the ship, for he was a sailor and knew her worth; and he was impressed by the skipper, the big, bluff Newfoundlander named Bob Bartlett, who grabbed his hand warmly and shouted, "By God, she's a ship, Henson! You ever see one finer? The best damn ice ship a mother's son ever keeled. Am I right?"

"You're right," Henson agreed.

"And I hear you're the best damn dogteam driver in the North," Bartlett boomed generously.

"I heard you're the best damn skipper afloat," Henson said with a grin.

Bartlett roared with laughter and clapped Henson on the back. "By God, I see we agree on everything!" And they were friends.

It was well, for there was to be plenty of grounds for friction between these two. Peary was to demote Henson and make Bartlett his right-hand man on this expedition. Peary still clung to his Victorian concepts of courage—it was the gentleman who must have it in greatest abundance. Captain Bob Bartlett was not a gentleman, but he *was* white and that made him closer to a gentleman than the black man. Peary was not acting on prejudice per se; he was doing what he thought best for the success of the expedition. He would allow no sentiment or loyalties to stand between him and the North Pole.

Not once during the coming year did Henson show the slightest resentment; not once did he give less than his total best. His friends back home would have railed at his passivity, but they would have misunderstood. He, too, was committed to reaching the Pole. It was not within him to shirk or sulk. Still there rose in him a foreboding, a premonition of failure. Never before had he experienced this emotion, and he searched for its roots, eager to cut them off and be rid of the feeling.

This was the most lavishly equipped expedition of all. They were sailing north in a stout boat especially designed for the job ahead, and the experience of all the previous efforts would save them from many errors. All the omens were favorable, so what was the source of this strange and unwelcome mood?

He suddenly realized with great shock that it was Peary! The commander of the expedition was a tired and sick man!

Eighteen years in the North had scarred him. He had not fully recovered from the operation on his feet. Over the past months he had relentlessly stumped the country in a search for funds to build the *Roosevelt* and take her north. He had committed every penny of his own: all the royalties from his writings, all the fees from his lectures. He had won the battle but at great cost in his own substance.

As the *Roosevelt* sailed out of New York he stood on her bridge, erect, proud, and determined, but his face was lined with fatigue and his eyes seemed incapable of the old fires. The men standing around him were unaware of the change, for they were strangers. Only Henson knew. Only Henson had the premonition of failure.

The expedition was beset by accidents almost from the beginning. Captain Bob Bartlett kept a log in which he recorded the first one:

"By the time we got to Etah . . . the rotten whale meat we had taken on down on the Labrador coast had seeped into the vessel's timbers all along the main deck. Then one of our Eskimos knocked out his pipe and the first thing we knew the ship was on fire. It was bad enough to have her burning up but the smell of the smoldering whale blubber was enough to asphyxiate one. After a fight we got it out."[29]

From Etah the *Roosevelt* moved into the Robeson Channel where a sudden swirl of the current drove her against two big floes, grinding her stern on the ice foot. Within minutes the back of the rudder had been twisted on its stock, the heavy head-band fittings had been broken, and the steel tiller rods snapped. She was able to limp into Cape Brevoort on the northern side of New-man Bay where a week was spent in repairs.

With half her boilers leaking and useless the *Roosevelt* finally did batter her way to the northern shore of Grant Land and the following March Peary was ready to conquer the Polar ice cap. But it was not as he had anticipated; it was not an unbroken, homogeneous ice field, not a level, slightly drifting snow plain stretched away to infinity in the north. It was a crushing, grind-ing, moving field of drift ice, at rest neither in winter nor summer. The entire Polar ice cap rotates across the top of the world from west to east, the ice forming on the northern shores of Siberia and moving across into the North Atlantic and then pouring south-ward between Spitzbergen and Greenland. The result of all this movement is the building of incalculable pressures that send the ice floes shooting up in enormous pressure ridges fifty or sixty feet high. All this chaotic ice is separated from the foot ice that extends from land by a "big lead," an open river of water, that alternately freezes and thaws as the ice north of it moves eastward.

Peary was unprepared for this mountainous travel. The expe-dition began the march north on March 2, 1906. A month and a half later it had made it to 87 degrees, 6 minutes north latitude, an all-time record. But he was still 174 miles from his goal. He could go no farther.

On April 21 he entered in his journal: ". . . as I looked at the drawn faces of my comrades, the skeleton figures of my few re-maining dogs, at my nearly empty sledges, and remembered the drifting ice over which we had come, and the unknown quantity of the Big Lead between us and the nearest land, I felt that I had cut the margin as narrow as could be reasonably expected. I told my men we should turn back from here."[30]

On the return trip they failed to take into account that the Polar cap on which they stood was rotating to the east, and when they finally were able to cross the Big Lead they found their trail gone. They were north of Greenland instead of north of Grant Land where the ship awaited them. They had the greatest difficulty in convincing the Eskimos that safety lay to the west, not to the south.

The return to the ship of the beaten, half-dead expedition was not the winning of rest and safety. Disaster dogged them as the *Roosevelt* headed south through the Robeson and Kennedy Channels. They were wrapped round with constant storms and an almost continuous series of breakdowns. The topmast and rigging were carried away; heavy seas struck the starboard quarter and broke the rudder stock square off, leaving the ship drifting helplessly. A jury rudder was rigged from a spar, only to have that carried away. The storm increased to hurricane violence and continued for thirty-six hours. When it abated, a second jury rudder was rigged after two days' work, with the crew being flung about the ship by the quixotic winds. Again under way, they made a new rudder from one of the ship's beams, and when the gale had blown itself out, the new rudder was hung.

Now they had run out of fuel and had to forage ashore for it, using spruce wood to replace the coal. When the spruce was gone they burned blubber. When the blubber was gone they began to burn the interior posts of the ship herself. It was now a question whether they could reach safe harbor before the ship cannibalized herself to the bottom of the sea. The *Roosevelt* made Battle Harbor, Labrador, on November 2, only to have heavy winds attack her and part the lines that moored her to the shore. The ring bolts were pulled out of her deck and the stock of the 2,000-pound anchor broken. She almost went ashore to end her brief, battle-scarred career, but the crew was able to keep her afloat.

On Christmas Eve, 1906 she made it back to New York. The return voyage had occupied seven months and was to become a classic of the sea. Men who later visited her in dry dock, and saw the almost mortal damage to her sternposts and rudder, found it difficult to believe that a ship in that condition could have made such a voyage.

It was dramatically proper that the final trip north should have been the most difficult of all, fitting that Peary and Henson should end their careers with the greatest display of courage and fortitude. So the public said. If Peary could not reach the North Pole, no man could. Give an old man all honor for attempting the impossible. So the editorials read.

Then Peary said to the reporters, "We are back for repairs and supplies."

The reporters were incredulous. "You mean you're going back?" they demanded.

"As soon as we're outfitted," Peary snapped. "Next summer, at the latest. And this time I'll nail the Stars and Stripes to the North Pole."

When this news was headlined across the nation, the public was awed. They admired Peary, of course, but they thought he must be slightly mad.

Alone with Henson, Peary dropped his heroic posture and said, "Matt, this trip will be our last. Win or lose, we can never go north again."

They were prophetic words.

[XVI]

Henson and Peary faced the last great adventure quite differently. They were, of course, quite different men, and all the years of intimacy and dependence upon each other had not bridged the class and racial chasm between them. But also, they had altered much since they first met twenty years before.

Peary had started out with a purpose, ribbed and edged with steel. Now it had become a passion. There was every reason not to attempt the Pole again. His own scarred and crippled fifty-two-year-old body was reason; the record of failure, not alone his but of every man who had attempted the Pole, was reason; his lonely, long-deserted, and very anxious family was reason—but he was beyond reason. He wished for either victory or death. There was no doubt that within the year he would win one or the other.

Henson, on the other hand, had started out with nothing but a passion for adventure, but this had been fired into firm purpose. He wanted to prove that a Negro could match a white man in facing and surmounting vicissitudes. He did not wish to die in the process, for that would not be the proof. His wish to live was shown by his last act before going north: he married young Lucy Ross.

Personnel for the expedition had to be recruited all over again.

Only two men had ever gone a second time on a Polar expedition with Peary and Henson; none a third. Each expedition had to be staffed with amateurs. This time Peary reverted to type: he surrounded himself with college men. Despite experience, he could not rid himself of the conviction that gentlemen were the bravest.

Besides the twenty-two crew members of the *Roosevelt*, the expedition was to consist of George Borup, just graduated from Yale University; Ross G. Marvin, instructor at Cornell University; Dr. J. W. Goodsell, with a degree from Pulte Medical College; Donald B. MacMillan, graduate of Peary's own alma mater, Bowdoin, and a teacher at Worcester (Massachusetts) Academy; and those two non-gentlemen, Captain Bob Bartlett and Matthew Henson. As it turned out, the college men did not this time disillusion Peary; they had courage and will power to the full measure. If Peary failed it would be for no reason of dereliction by these men.

Knowing this was his last effort, Peary made his preparations with cold and desperate efficiency. He spent months over the logistics of the expedition, knew what was necessary to be done almost to each day of each month. Henson and Charlie Percy, the cook, lived aboard the *Roosevelt* at dock to direct the stowage of supplies.

The lazaretto (between decks) was arsenal of the ship, holding ammunition and guns, powder to make ammunition, dynamite for blasting ice. Here also was stowed tobacco, alcohol, picks and shovels, carpenter's and tinsmith's tools for Henson. Into the after hold went jam, beans, canned fruit, candy, 16,000 pounds of flour, 10,000 pounds of sugar, 10,000 pounds of biscuits, 7,000 pounds of bacon, 3,500 gallons of kerosene, 3,000 pounds of dried fish, 1,000 pounds of coffee, 800 pounds of tea, 100 cases of condensed milk, and, most important of all, 30,000 pounds of pemmican to be used on the trail. The pemmican came in blue tins for humans and red tins for the dogs. The dogs were to learn the significance of the colors, and whenever they broke loose aboard ship or on the trail, they made for the red tins and ripped them open with their teeth.

Also taken aboard were magazines, five cases of books, elaborate photography supplies including complete darkroom equipment, field glasses and sunglasses, maps and charts, theodolites, sextants, thermometers, tidal gauges, compasses. There were warm clothes, but not those that would be worn on the trail. The expedition would be dressed exactly as the Eskimos dressed, and their clothes would be made in the North during the long winter night by the Eskimo women.

And there was coal in every available inch of hold and deck space that was left. The *Roosevelt's* great failing was excessive consumption of coal. She had engines of 1,000 horsepower, of the inverted compound type, two water tubes, and one Scotch boiler, all to drive a single eleven-foot propeller. She was strong, she could steam and she could sail, but she could not leave any port in the United States and steam to the shore of the Polar ice cap and reach home again with the coal in her bunkers. Thus the auxiliary ship *Erik* had been chartered to follow her and refuel her in the North.

As the *Roosevelt* began to take on supplies in New York the public interest rose. It was an interest compounded of hero worship, compassion, and some ghoulishness. Henson felt it in some of his friends. When they would sit together over coffee in the Harlem apartments, they hung on every detail of the ship and equipment, urged him to assure them that the expedition would succeed. But when he did, they mentally shook their heads and returned to eager questioning, wanting to store up details for future memories of a doomed expedition.

As a result of the widely held belief that this was a quixotic adventure that could not possibly succeed, crackpot suggestions flooded the *Roosevelt*. They amused Henson, who used to quote them to the rest of the crew.

One day when Peary came aboard for his usual inspection, Henson met him at the gangplank, waved a letter, and exclaimed, "We've wasted a lot of time and money, Commander. We don't need to take all these food supplies north. There's a better way."

"What this time, Matt?" Peary said with a grin.

"A soup pipeline! This guy sent us blueprints and specifications and everything. All we have to do is to install an enormous soup boiler on the *Roosevelt*. Then, as we advance over the ice cap, we lay pipe every inch of the way, and the boiler forces hot soup through the pipe to us, right to the North Pole."

Peary appeared to study the idea for a moment, then announced, "Only one drawback, Matt."

"What can that be?" Henson was amazed.

"I don't like soup."

Henson shrugged and dropped the letter over the side.

In another mail there arrived a detailed plan to equip a boat with a bow that got red-hot so it could melt a path to the Pole. One elaborate drawing revealed a specially designed mobile head-quarters to be used on the ice. It was a knock-down house, ten by twelve feet, containing a set of tanks filled with hydrogen gas. In the center was a small engine that caused a heavy chain loop to revolve out through a front window, along the surface of the ice like the tread of a tractor, and back in through a rear window. When it came time to advance, the gas was fed into a balloon on the roof of the structure, the balloon raised the house two feet off the ice, the engine was started, and the chain tractor began to move, pulling the slightly levitated structure forward. The expedition could travel to the Pole without ever stepping outdoors!

While the supplies were being taken aboard, the new members of the expedition came, one at a time, to see their quarters and install their personal belongings. Young Donald MacMillan, who, years later, was to become a renowned Arctic explorer on his own, wrote about his first visit to the *Roosevelt*:

I first met Matt Henson aboard the Commander's steamer *Roosevelt*, being loaded with equipment at a New York dock. I climbed over the rail and was surveying the ship's facilities for the first time, when a stateroom door opened and out he stepped with hand extended in greeting and a ready smile. I recognized him from newspaper photographs.

"Glad to meet you, professor," he said, and he gave me the title thereafter, although I was no more than a preparatory school instructor. About five feet eight inches, black-haired and clean-shaven, he was a handsome fellow and although an athlete myself, I watched with admiration the ease with which he moved and worked about the ship; he was obviously in splendid condition.

We sat on the caplog and he talked about the Arctic, of which I could not hear enough for what he already knew so well I was just beginning to learn. Since he was modest, it took me much longer to learn what his true role had been. . . . I did not then know that he was to teach me how to survive in the North.[31]

As the sailing date approached, greater and greater crowds came to the *Roosevelt's* dock to watch final preparations. There was much dockside discussion about the North Pole, none of it quite clear about the nature of the thing. Many thought it was a pole that stuck up in the air, probably striped, and that it would be removed by these brave men and returned to America for exhibition.

On July 6 the *Roosevelt* left her pier, and to the accompaniment of shouts and waved handkerchiefs and harbor whistles and horns, made her way up the East River. There was an important first stop at Oyster Bay, Long Island, for the President of the United States desired to come aboard his namesake. Teddy Roosevelt insisted on examining every inch of the ship, exclaiming "Bully!" over and over. He met and shook hands with every member of the expedition and crew, and expressed his envy of them on their great adventure.

Peary and Roosevelt stood together on deck as photographers took their pictures. Roosevelt said, "How I would like to go along!"

Peary replied, "Mr. President, I shall put into this effort everything there is in me—physical, mental, and moral."

Roosevelt grasped his hand and exclaimed, "I believe in you, Peary, and I believe in your success—if it is within the possibility of man."

That final qualification of the President's was shared by the nation.

During the voyage north, uneventful until the arrival at the whaling station at St. Charles, Labrador, the relationship of the men began to take form. If newcomers had expected intimacy and easy camaraderie with their commander, they were soon disabused. Peary retired into his cabin to remain there, remote and thoughtful. From time to time the members of the expedition would be called into his quarters for lectures and instructions, but Peary never came to their quarters for relaxation or companionship. His was the lonely desperation of a last battle.

Captain Bob Bartlett, skipper of the *Roosevelt* again for this expedition, was the most conspicuous man on the ship. He had a lean, weathered face with hawk-like nose above a drooping mustache. He came from a long line of Newfoundland sea captains and ruled his ship with loud, profane justice. He was intimidated by no man—not even Peary. He gave his loyalty to Peary because it was deserved, not commanded.

On one of his subsequent trips north he had Mrs. Peary and young teen-age Marie Peary as passengers. One evening bread pudding was the dessert, and when Marie put her spoon into it she came upon a cud of chewing tobacco. With Bartlett watching her sharply, Marie put the spoon down and pushed the pudding aside.

Bartlett pounded the table with his fist and shouted, "People who is fastidious should not go on Polar expeditions. Nobody expects ya to eat the chaw of tobacco, but, by God, there's nothin' wrong with the puddin'."

With Peary withdrawn and Bartlett busy with the running of the ship, the remaining members of the expedition were thrown together to speculate, anticipate. There was earnest and painstaking Ross G. Marvin, a veteran of the previous trip north on the *Roosevelt* and listed as Peary's personal secretary. He was to be murdered in the North. There was fleshy, ponderous Dr. J. W. Goodsell, who was not designed by nature to be very good on the Arctic trail but compensated by sheer determination. There was George Borup, the Yale athlete and perhaps the perfect shipmate because of his ebullient good humor. There was Donald B. MacMillan, who was quick and strong and cheerful and eager to learn. Of all the men, MacMillan gave the greatest promise of mastering the skills of the trail.

Henson marked him at once and confided to his journal, which he now began to keep, "I am going to cultivate his acquaintance."[32]

Then there was, of course, Henson himself. But he was so self-effacing that the rest of the expedition was hardly aware of him during those early days of the voyage. When they hit their first storm, however, they suddenly realized he was aboard.

MacMillan later wrote:

I remember very well an 80-mile-an-hour gale in Buchanan Bay aboard the *Roosevelt*. Sheets of solid, ice-cold spray poured over the bow, sluiced everything over the rail that wasn't tied down, and made it hazardous to stay anywhere on deck. The steamer was lunging and laboring into green-gray head seas and the heavy motion of her pitch threatened to smash the whaleboats, which were jumping in the davits.

For the next hour, Matt was all over that ship, virtually unmindful of his own safety, acting with a sailor's instinct and without orders, which could not have been heard in the wind anyway, he worked taking in sail and securing the boats with the vigor of three men.[33]

And so these men became acquainted, each measuring and weighing with the knowledge that his own life was largely in his comrades' hands.

Among the things these eager young men learned during the early days of the voyage was that their new world was to smell differently from their accustomed one. The *Roosevelt* put in at a whaling station just below Battle Harbor, Labrador, to take on 30,000 pounds of old whale meat. This would be food for the Eskimo dogs they would pick up in Greenland, and since the dogs weren't particular about the age of the meat, the food was cheap and ancient. The *Roosevelt* now began to reek so intensely that her presence would be announced to ships miles away across open water.

Later the *Roosevelt* put into Hawks Harbor and tied up near the immaculate yacht *Wakiva* out of New York. All the ladies and gentlemen aboard her were thrilled to see the famous expedition and sent word they would like to come aboard and meet the famous Commander Peary. Permission was given.

The whale meat was stowed on deck, and to save the visitors the necessity of wading through it, a boardwalk was laid upon the jellylike mass from the companion ladder to Peary's cabin door. When the visitors arrived, dressed in yachting whites, they paused at the top of the companionway, their faces aghast. They considered letting Peary sail on north without their good wishes, but finally overcame this unworthy impulse and stepped out onto the planking. It jiggled and swayed and threatened to throw them into the decaying, blubberous mass, but never quite did.

They shook Peary's hand briefly and left the ship with all haste. Back in New York they were heard to brag of their bravery.

On August 1 the *Roosevelt* put in at Cape York, Greenland. It was here that the expedition would select and take aboard the Eskimos and their dogs. Though there was a blizzard at the time of arrival, the Eskimo men came out in their kayaks to shout:

"Pearyaksoah! Miy Paluk! Pearyaksoah! Miy Paluk!"

Peary and Henson leaned over the rail to wave in response to the warm greetings. When they finally dropped anchor and went ashore in a whaleboat, the entire village danced happily around them. The greenhorns on the trip were amazed at the affection shown both Peary and Henson, realizing it spoke well for a relationship of honest dealing that had extended between the explorers and this tribe of Smith Sound aborigines for over twenty years.

It was soon obvious that Peary was respected and obeyed by these small brown people, but Henson was loved. Old friends vied with each other to have him sleep in their igloos, to feed him, to make new clothing for him. There was Kudlooktoo, his son, now grown to manhood, who walked possessively beside him; there were Sipsoo and Seegloo and Ootah, but, sadly, no Ahnalka. He had died.

Peary delegated to Henson the job of selecting the personnel and the dogs to make the trip to the Arctic. With an instinct born of long experience, Matt selected and bought (with guns and ammunition and cooking utensils) the best dogs of the tribe, but when it came to choosing the men and women, his job was most difficult. Not that he didn't know who was best; he hated to hurt the feelings of those who were second-rate.

In the midst of the process the *Erik* arrived, bringing a New Haven sportsman named Harry Whitney, who proposed to spend the winter on Greenland, hunting game. Henson and a few Eskimos took Whitney on a walrus hunt and he proved an apt student.

The *Roosevelt* moved north to Etah, there to take on more Eskimos and dogs. On August 18 the ship sailed out of Etah and headed north into the ice pack of the Kane Basin. The last vestige of civilization, of human habitation, was now left behind.

Peary wrote: "Behind me now lay everything that was mine, everything that a man personally loves, family, friends, home and all those hundreds of associations which linked me with my kind. Ahead of me lay my dream, my destiny, the goal of that ir-resistible impulsion which had driven me for 23 years to hurl myself, time after time, against the frigid *NO* of the Great North."[34]

Captain Bob Bartlett also wrote of this day, but his words lacked the mysticism of Peary's. He observed:

. . . Mixed up with the coal were 70 tons of whale meat and 246 dogs, all fighting and screaming—the dogs, I mean. In addition we had 49 Eskimos and the blubber of 50 walruses. To get some idea of what this meant you must remember that the *Roosevelt* was not any bigger than the average tug. She was already weighted down with a heavy cargo of supplies and equipment for at least a year in the Far North. To my dying day I shall never forget the frightful noise, the choking stench and the terrible confusion that reigned aboard her as we steamed slowly down Foulke Fjord and swung around into the pack of Kane Basin. We had some canned peaches for supper that night; but the odor about us was so powerful that the peaches simply felt wet and cold on one's tongue, having no fruit flavor whatsoever.[35]

There was soon more to be concerned about than the flavor of the peaches. The *Roosevelt* entered into a life-and-death struggle with the ice pack. She had penetrated through these waters on her previous trip, and that time she had almost been destroyed in the process. There was no assurance that she could repeat her performance. In fact, as the violence of the struggle increased, the whaleboats were provisioned and every man assigned a vital box of supplies and a spot on the railing where he should go over the side if the worst should happen. This stout boat suddenly seemed frail as she was put to the cruel ordeal.

With Captain Bartlett in the crow's nest screaming orders down to the helmsman, and Peary clinging to the rigging halfway up to observe, the ship was used as a battering ram against the ice, splitting the great cakes or forcing them aside. There were moments when she was caught in the relentless crush of the ice field, and then as the pressure against her sides mounted, her decks bulged upwards and the rigging slackened, and from the holds came loud reports, a fusillade, as the timbers cracked, and the whole ship quivered like a tight bowstring. But each time she was able to squeeze upward and leap from the death jaws, leaving in her wake a snarling turmoil of cheated ice.

Peary wrote:

The *Roosevelt* fought like a gladiator, turning, twisting, straining with all her force, smashing her full weight against the heavy floes whenever we could get room for a rush, and rearing upon them like a steeplechaser taking a fence. . . . The forward rush, the gathering speed and momentum, the crash, the upward heave, the grating snarl of the ice as the steel-shod stem split it as a mason's hammer splits granite, or trod it under, or sent it right and left in whirling fragments, followed by the violent roll, the backward rebound, and then the gathering for another rush . . . At such times everyone on deck hung with breathless interest in our movement, and as Bartlett and I clung to the rigging I heard him whisper through teeth clenched from the purely physical tension of the throbbing ship under us: "Give it to 'em, Teddy, give it to 'em."[36]

Throughout it all was the frightening knowledge that each mile achieved northward removed them just that much farther from home, was a mile that would have to be fought all over again on the return trip—*if* there was a return trip.

Tortuously northward they went through the Kennedy and Robeson Channels. On September 5, after almost a month of struggle, they came to the edge of the Polar Sea and found a small lead of open water between foot ice and sea ice. The "ice foot" is formed by the rise and fall of the tides working against the shoreline. Each time the tide falls it leaves a thin deposit of water on the shore which then freezes and extends into the sea. If a ship is not of heavy draft she can steam along the shore between the ice foot and the heavy sea ice. This was what the *Roosevelt* now did, making her way to Cape Sheridan, the site of Peary's 1906 winter quarters.

During the previous expedition the *Roosevelt* had been berthed in a precarious position and subjected to attack by tides and ice, so now every effort was made to get her into shallow water and close to shore, safe from the hostile pack outside.

This having been accomplished, even further precautions were taken; vital equipment was removed from the boat and placed on land. Peary wrote: "With the supplies ashore, the loss of the ship by fire or by crushing in the ice would mean simply that the men would have to walk home. It would not interfere with the sledge work, nor seriously cripple the expedition."[37]

[XVII]

The long night now descended upon them. This was a period dreaded by explorers, a period when men's nerves gave way. It had been the policy of all other northern expeditions to hole in during the long night, to try and fight off the oppression of darkness by all sorts of games and amateur theatricals. *Never* was any serious exploration made until the terror was gone and the sun returned in the spring.

Not so with the Peary expeditions. The Arctic night was a period of intense activity during which all equipment was made, repaired, and used in practice operations. No theatricals were ever performed in a Peary camp; there wasn't time.

Cape Sheridan was at 82 degrees, 28 minutes north latitude, and on December 22, the middle of the long night, the sun would be 15 degrees, 48 minutes below the horizon. This means that there remained a glimmer of twilight on the southern horizon, except, of course, on stormy days. Still, the disappearance of the sun affected all men, white and Eskimo alike.

Even Peary was touched by the night moods. He wrote: "Mingled with the work and plans and anxieties were times for thoughts and impressions . . . as much a part of the Arctic night as the ice, the darkness and the cold. Moments of exultation and moments of depression. Moments of eager impatience when I wished that the day for the departure north might be tomorrow. Moments of foreboding when I dreaded the arrival. Moments of sanguine hopes, others of darkest misgivings . . ."[38]

It was during the Arctic night that mutinies festered and broke open in other expeditions. Explorer Charles Francis Hall shot two of his men; one man was shot by Greely; Dr. Elisha Kent Kane shot one of his men but missed. Mutiny became such a common occurrence that the British Admiralty ruled that all Arctic expeditions should be under military discipline.

There were no mutinies at Cape Sheridan. Not only was there too much work to allow it, but there was the presence of Matthew Henson. During the winter Matt became the mainspring of the camp. He was everywhere, teaching, encouraging, working tirelessly and with inexhaustible good humor.

The first thing Henson undertook was the construction of the sledges. Of all the equipment, the sledge was probably the most important and the most temperamental. It had to combine lightness with strength and easy traction. Every detail of it was of the utmost importance and the slightest change could alter its effectiveness, just as the change of a ship's lines could slow her speed. Peary had designed a sledge that differed from the traditional Eskimo ones, but it was Henson who built them.

It was put together, not with nails and screws, but with sealskin rawhide lashings. These gave it flexibility. The runners were longer than those on the Eskimo sledge, and curved up at both ends to allow easier passage over rough ice. The greenhorns on the expedition watched Henson at work and were amazed at his skill as he constructed two dozen sledges. MacMillan wrote:

The Eskimos would gather about when Matt put a sledge together, watching his skill, but waiting particularly for one part of the operation. In lashing together a sledge, a white man braces his foot on the sledge, leans back and pulls the rawhide taut with both hands. When Henson did it, he would bend down, seize the bight of the rawhide in his powerful white teeth, pull back his head until the cords on his strong neck stood out, then deftly make fast the lashing. The Eskimos would shake their heads and grunt approval. That was their way of doing it and this fellow of the South . . . did a good job, too. Even the oldtimers would run their hands over the lashings, look in, under, and about to make certain everything was just so, and say, "*Ajungilak*" (it is good).[39]

Next to sledges, the most important item of equipment was clothing. Peary and Henson had learned that there was no choice between woolens and nature's gift to the animals, fur. They had learned to dress as the Eskimos dressed, and there was just no improvement civilization could make. Under Henson's foremanship the Eskimo women made the clothing for the white men, as well as for their own husbands. They chewed each piece of hide to make it flexible before stitching it into garments, and by middle age they generally had worn their teeth down to the gums. Still, this was the badge of a good and industrious wife and was displayed with pride.

Socks were made of Arctic hare, fur next to the feet. Kamiks, or boots, were of sealskin or fur from the legs of reindeer, bear, or musk ox. Henson instructed all the greenhorns to put a nest of grass in the bottom of the kamik on which the sock rested, for this helped to absorb the moisture and keep the feet warm. By changing the grass every two or three days a man could use a pair of kamiks much longer before drying them over a stove.

From just below the knees up to the waist were pants made of bearskin, since this is the only fur that is almost as warm wet as dry. The quality of the bearskin in a man's pants was a status symbol among the Eskimos. The polar bear is the fiercest, strongest, best-adapted animal in the North. He doesn't hibernate; he's up and out in all kinds of weather, asking no quarter, plodding through the darkness and the storm, surviving in all temperatures. The only thing that keeps him from the North Pole is the absence of food. It took a brave and skillful hunter to bring down a polar bear, and thus his hide was prized as a garment.

Above the waist was a kooletah, a shirt made of deerskin with the sleeves large so the arms could be withdrawn and warmed on the belly. Above it was a hood made of bearskin or a deerskin roll. In case of wind this could be drawn over the head and around the face. The back of it was very loose, to allow a continual stream of cold air to circulate up and down the body and remove any moisture from perspiration.

These garments could be transformed into a sleeping bag by the simple procedure of drawing the kooletah tight at the waist and passing a string between the legs to hold it in position, at the same time tightening the strings at the top of the kamiks and pulling the hands from the sleeves to place them inside on the belly.

"Never stand with your hands on your hips," Henson warned his pupils. "You never see an Eskimo stand that way, and for a good reason. Such a position lets a lot of air pass between the body and the arms, and you get chilled. Let your arms drop at your sides and you'll be warmer.

"When you're on the trail and living in igloos," Matt continued, "you'll rise in the morning to find your kamiks are moist and soft from the condensation around your feet. When you first step outside, stand quietly for a time, make very little movement. This will let the kamiks freeze to the shape of your feet for the day's march. If you walk before they are frozen, they will freeze in awkward positions and you'll develop blisters."

The men nodded soberly. They were learning, not just the art of travel and comfort, but the grim business of survival. Matt continued, "Every day inspect all your garments for tiny holes or tears. A rip will mean a spot of frozen flesh even before you feel the cold.

"And if you freeze a part of your body, *warm* it. Somehow the story got around that when an Eskimo freezes his foot he rubs it with snow. Well, snow at fifty degrees below zero would just freeze his foot that much harder. What he really does is put it against his wife's warm belly."

Of equal importance with clothing was shelter on the trail. Peary and Henson had started out their careers using tents, but had given them up in favor of the Eskimo shelter, a snow igloo. The igloo is a perfect protection against snow and wind, it conserves the fuel that must be carried on the sledges, and it eliminates the weight of the tent which must also be carried. To unbend a frozen tent, hitting it and kicking it into shape with chilled fists and feet, setting it up against a wind that may be so strong that a man hardly can stand against it, is difficult work at best. Add to that the fact that by the end of a trip a tent has doubled and trebled its weight with ice as a result of condensation of the steam from cooking pots and moisture from human breath, and the disadvantages of a tent become obvious. The Eskimo way was the best.

Henson and two Eskimos now began to teach the members of the expedition how to construct igloos. The one indispensable tool was a snow knife. It was about the size of a machete but the leading edge was serrated so that the frozen snow could be sawed. The snow blocks were, roughly, 24" x 18" x 6", and were laid in a circle, spirally, counterclockwise. Each block was held by the left hand and cut and fitted into position by the right. Since each spiraling row is cut slightly smaller than the last, the igloo comes to a rounded dome top, leaving a final hole to be filled in by a block cut to fit. Entrance was by a tunnel dug from the outside and under the wall of the igloo to the inside, thus trapping warm air within.

"The igloo is never allowed to get really warm," Henson explained, "because if it did it would begin to melt and drip water all over our clothes. We control the temperature by opening and closing the hole in the roof. The temperature, aside from when we cook, depends upon the body heat of the people in the igloo; four people can raise the temperature fifteen degrees."

"Matt," Borup interrupted, "you mean that if it is fifty degrees below zero outside, our bodies will warm the igloo to only thirty-five degrees below zero?"

"Exactly," Matt said. Then with a grin, "That's plenty warm for a good sleep on the trail."

He was kidding because, as he explained, they usually tried to get the temperature a little warmer than that.

"These igloos will be made at the end of each march toward

the Pole," Matt explained, "and then reoccupied on the return marches. If, however, we decide to live in a snow igloo for any length of time, we use the stove to heat the temperature above freezing. Then when the walls begin to run with water we kick out the top block and let the cold air rush in. This gives the inside walls a hard glaze and strengthens the igloo against storms."

The stove Matt referred to was of Peary's design and Matt's construction. The so-called Primus stove had been used by other explorers, but it was bulky and inefficient in contrast with the ones Matt had made for this expedition. With about eight ounces of fuel and an improved ice basket, it could create a gallon of boiling water in about twenty minutes. With less ice to be converted to water, supper could be prepared in half the time. The importance of the stove could not be underestimated. It might well mean the difference between success and failure on the trail, perhaps even between life and death.

As for the food, it was to be the simplest and the lightest. Basic was pemmican. This was an Indian word in Cree dialect, meaning "fatty food." Peary's pemmican was especially compounded and packaged, and was 62 percent ground beef and 38 percent suet with a dash of seasoning and raisins. It contained highly concentrated nutrition and, compared to other foods available in the North, was pleasant to the palate.

The basic liquid was tea. This was found to be better than coffee or chocolate for cold work because it warms a man faster, gives him a lift without any aftereffect. It is light to transport, easy to prepare. Science had determined that a man could live and work on Peary's basic daily ration: 16 ounces of pemmican (8 in the morning and 8 in the evening), 16 ounces of biscuits, 4 ounces of condensed milk, 1½ ounces of compressed tea. Here were the necessary proteins, fats, and carbohydrates—enough to get a man to the North Pole and back, all other conditions being fortunate.

The dog ration was also pemmican of a slightly different formula, each dog receiving one pound per day. With eight dogs to a sledge, the sledge carried supplies of one 8-pound can of dog pemmican per day. Each block of the frozen food was scored into eight parts to make it easy to parcel out the meals.

For all the careful advance preparation, for all Peary's and Henson's cumulative wisdom gained over twenty years in the North, one vital aspect of the expedition now had to start from scratch—the greenhorns had to be turned into dogteam drivers. It was the most difficult of all the northern skills, and the most vital.

In these expeditions the dogs were *driven;* there was no lead dog to select a path and spring down it. The eight dogs were fastened to the sledge in fan shape and it was up to the driver to select and force the direction and speed. Also, the weight of the loaded sledges was not calculated to the strength of the eight dogs, but to the strength of the dogs *plus* that of the driver. If a sledge is deep in snow, or locked against a pressure ridge, the dogs cannot start it moving alone; it is up to the driver to lift and push and obtain momentum before the dogs take over.

Here again it was Henson who taught the others. His students, strong and intelligent and well-coordinated men, had the usual difficulties. Both George Borup and Donald MacMillan were eager to learn and certain they would quickly master the art. Henson started out with Borup on a practice run and everything was going fine, but the moment Henson stepped aside, the dogs slowed down and finally just stopped and sat in the snow. "The twenty-five foot whip was tried [by me]," Borup wrote, "but the dogs never moved. They certainly were amused at the exhibition I put up. First thing I did was to sting myself a crack in the face, then I knocked my hat off. On the third try I managed to miss myself but hit an Eskimo who was passing. Next time the lash snarled around a dog trace."[40]

Finally, in desperation, Borup grabbed up a snowshoe and began to hit the dogs on their rumps. They moved a few feet, then sat down again to stare at him resentfully.

The twenty-five-foot whip was the key to success, Matt explained to Borup. He demonstrated how to handle it, time after time hitting a predetermined spot the size of a quarter. Affectionately rubbing the head of the king dog, he said, "You don't have to hit them with the whip, but you have to let them know you *can* hit them if necessary. A crack of the whip just a few inches above their heads is sufficient. But if they find you can't do it, you might as well give up. They'll never obey you."

MacMillan wrote of Henson: ". . . without profanity or brutality, with little more than a movement of the arm or wrist, with all the proficiency of a skillful fly fisherman, he piloted his cumbersome command over the craggy sea ice while lesser men covered fewer miles and had more accidents."[41]

So through the night Henson taught the necessary skills. The lessons were received in dead seriousness, for the men's lives depended upon the learning. November, December, January passed. MacMillan and Marvin took tidal observations; Henson led the hunting parties; Bartlett cared for the ship and commanded the crew. Borup was a gadfly who eagerly participated in everything; Goodsell treated frostbite and stomach upsets and piblokto and all the other ailments of the flesh; Peary spent hours in his cabin, brooding over charts as he checked and rechecked and checked again his tactics for the Polar Sea. All he had learned and suffered in a lifetime was brought to bear on this final problem of how to leave land and travel over 400 miles of Polar Sea with no life upon it, reach the Pole and travel the 400 miles in return. Peary had once seen the footprint of a polar bear, but never actually seen a living thing and he had to proceed on the assumption there was none.

He could not lay down caches of food. On Greenland they had been snowed under; on the Polar Sea they had drifted with the ice pack—in both cases, lost. There was no game to be shot between his winter headquarters and the Pole; therefore, all food had to be carried on a sledge. Yet, even with the most ruthless elimination of nonessential items, a man and team couldn't carry enough food to feed themselves for the 800-mile march. And to add another sledge was to add more men and dogs and, therefore, more mouths to be fed. It seemed a vicious circle. But Peary believed he had it broken.

On his last two expeditions he had devised and was now per-
fecting a system of supporting parties. In January he called the
members of his expedition together to go over the details of this
plan. It was a model of simplicity, yet required the highest degree
of coordination.

Each man (seven of them including Peary) was to be in command of a sub-party of two Eskimos, three sledges, and twenty-
four dogs. Each sub-party would be completely self-sufficient in
food, weapons, tools, and clothes, but would also carry extra
food sufficient to feed the combined parties for five days. All
seven parties would start out on the ice cap simultaneously, and
for the first five marches all would eat the supplies of a single
sub-party. At the end of that time, the sub-party, with emergency rations and a light sledge, would make double marches for
shore. Thereafter, each sub-party would feed the expedition for
five days, before returning to shore. By the time the sixth party
turned back a month later, Peary should be within striking distance of the Pole with his own party's rations untouched.

The men and dogs to turn back each time would be determined
on the spot, the weaker returning and the stronger going forward.
By this process Peary would always have available the pick of
men and dogs. Who would finally accompany him to the Pole,
no one knew, not even Peary, though he seemed to have a prefer-
ence for MacMillan—the Bowdoin man.

After explaining the plan to the members of the expedition,
Peary faced the more difficult task of explaining it to the Eskimos.
They had a great fear of the Polar ice cap where the evil spirit
Tahnusuk lived. All through the winter night Henson had been
cajoling, reassuring, kidding, promising, but they remained ap-
prehensive. Peary had a final argument, which he now used. First
he laid out a display of equipment on the mess-room table, then
covered it with a sheet and told Henson to summon the Eskimos.
They trooped in and stood around the table, wives slightly behind husbands.

Peary held up twenty-one matches in his hand, each match
representing a sledge and team and driver. Putting the matches on

the edge of the table, he aimed them toward a bottle standing in the middle. He then advanced all the matches five inches toward the bottle. Three of the matches were returned to the starting point. Peary advanced the rest of them another five inches. Then another three were returned, while the rest advanced again. This continued until there were only three or four matches making it all the way to the bottle.

The weakest men would be sent back on each returning party, Peary explained, and when they got back they could live on the ship and not have to go out on the sea again. However, four Eskimos would go all the way to the Pole with him. And he now wanted to show what each of these four men would receive. He whipped off the white cloth and a gasp of astonishment went up from the Eskimos. There on the table were two rifles, one shotgun, all kinds of knives, lance heads, shot and powder and reloading equipment, tobacco, oil, wood for sledges. And in addition to all this, each man would receive a whaleboat.

The men were thrilled, but the widest eyes and the biggest grins were on the wives' faces. It was obvious they would urge on their husbands.

The final land camp, the actual jumping-off place onto the sea, was to be Cape Columbia, a promontory about seventy-five miles northwest of the *Roosevelt* at Cape Sheridan. The sun had not yet come up over the horizon, and using lanterns to light the way, Bartlett started out with an advance division on February 15. The others followed shortly after, Peary coming last. When he approached Cape Columbia he met Borup and MacMillan on the trail, and each was surprised at the other. Peary had shaved off his famous walrus mustache, as he always did on the trail, and it was startling to see him without it for the first time.

Peary took a look at them and said briskly, "Borup, your face is frozen." Then turning to MacMillan, he added, "MacMillan, your nose is gone."

MacMillan felt his face, and his nose was still in place but hard as a block of wood. "How cold is it, Commander?" he asked.

"About fifty-seven below," Peary said.

This final land camp seethed with activity. Sledges were bottoms-up, their runners being burnished and their lashing checked; parted traces were being repaired; Henson, the only tinsmith, was soldering fuel tins that had been punctured on the rough trip from Cape Sheridan; six dogs had died from throat distemper on the march and the survivors were being sorted into the most effective teams; two Eskimos had become incapacitated, one with a frozen heel and the other with a swollen knee, and the supporting divisions were being reorganized.

Through it all they kept looking at the horizon, waiting for the sun. The dawn of the long Arctic day was dangerous because there were no shadows, and without them, men and dogs often failed to see holes and crevasses. It would be almost another two weeks before they moved out. And during this time the men worked under the tension imposed upon them by the vast stretches of ice rubble to the north. The Eskimos whispered to each other with dread.

March 1 was the last possible date to leave, according to Peary's calculations, and during the final week of February he and Henson scanned the north horizon for the dreaded "water sky." The moment the sun was full up open leads of water would increase, their presence indicated by a cloud above them. These were the most dangerous hazards, and yet they could not be avoided by wintertime travel because of winter's absence of light. It was Peary's hope to get to the Pole and back before the full summer sun created sufficient open water to trap them.

On the evening of February 27 Peary called the expedition to his igloo for a final briefing. This meant they were to start on the next day. Now that the moment was here, each man reacted according to his own nature and his own need. Peary, whose need was the greatest, so great in fact as to border on the pathological, responded with merciless self-discipline. In coldly scientific words he laid out the problems and the measures they would take to meet them. He did not minimize; he admitted to past failures and mistakes, but expressed the utmost confidence in their abilities to make this expedition a success. There was no pep talk, no razzle-dazzle, no attempt to find inspiration in mysticism, and yet he *did* inspire the men. His own confidence in the face of the frightening logic of their position made his subordinates believe in success.

After an hour of quiet talk he dismissed them. They drifted across the frozen, surrealist landscape in ones and twos, then entered Bartlett's igloo. They found it impossible to sleep immediately, and so in Bartlett's igloo they broke out a bottle of brandy and had a drink. They began to talk excitedly, their buoyant spirits no longer held in check by the realism of the commander.

Henson sat back and did not join in the eager talk. Tomorrow was to bring no new adventure for him, and he felt an emotion apparently unshared by these young men—fear. Delay always infected him with this sickening mood, and he knew from experience that once he was on the trail, when things began to happen, he would shed the fear and lose himself in a trance of action. But tonight there was the old feeling of emptiness in the pit of his stomach.

Then, suddenly, an amazing thing happened before his eyes. Young George Borup jumped to his feet, clutched his fists in front of him as if he were going to strike someone, then opened his mouth and let out a blood-curdling cry. This amazing sound was followed by a rapid sequence of consonants, then a rackety-rack, and a siss-boom-bah! He was giving a college yell!

Everyone laughed and clapped his hands, and now the others were encouraged to perform. MacMillan sang the Bowdoin college song. Then Marvin, in a clear, true voice, sang:

> Far above Cayuga's waters
> With its waves of blue,
> Stands our noble Alma Mater,
> Glorious to view.
> Lift the chorus, speed it onward,
> Loud her praises tell;
> Hail to thee, our Alma Mater,
> Hail, oh hail, Cornell!

After Goodsell had sung his school song, Borup bounced up again and began Yale's "Whiffenpoof Song." They all knew this and soon the measured chorus filled the igloo.

There was a sweet sadness about the song and as the last note lingered in the Arctic air, Henson could see that the men who had sung it were deeply moved. They were bound together by common memories and experiences that were somehow distilled in this little song. None of these emotions or memories could be shared by Henson, and he slipped quietly out of the igloo and walked slowly toward his own cold bed. On the way he passed Peary's igloo, and there was a light still burning within. He guessed what was now happening.

Peary had stripped to the waist and around his torso he was wrapping an old, patched piece of silk. It was an American flag, but not just any American flag. This one had been made by his wife years before and he had carried it wrapped around his body on every Arctic expedition. Pieces of it had been cut out and left under rocks at the northern terminus of each trip, and now the flag was patched in a half-dozen places. He had vowed he would carry this piece of silk to the North Pole.

Each man on the expedition had his own tribal sort of ritual to ease the weight of fear. Each man but Henson.

[XVIII]

Henson routed out the Eskimos with a shouted, "Ahdoolo! Ahdoolo!" It was his own made-up word that meant to get out of bed and go to work. Normally the Eskimos laughed when they heard the word, but this morning the laughter was short-lived, for they remembered that this was the day they were to venture onto the ice cap, the place they called Ser-mik-suah, the abode of evil spirits.

Henson gave them no time to brood on the fact; he was everywhere, giving orders, supervising the final hitching up of the dogteams. Within a short time everything was ready and Peary made a final inspection. Man and dog power did not conform to his precise plans, he found. Disease, normal wear and tear, and, in a few cases, malingering had reduced his complement but it was still adequate to the job. He was placing in the field twenty-two men and nineteen teams of seven dogs each.

The departure was quiet. There were no speeches, no waving and shouting. The fur-muffled figures took their positions behind their sledges, cracked their long whips and cried, "Huk! Huk!" And they moved off the land and onto the frozen sea. The course was a little west of true north, thus compensating for the easterly drift of the pack. The goal, beneath the North Star, was 400 miles away.

Bartlett and Borup were breaking trail and the main party followed their sledge tracks. The impress of steel sledge runners on
the compacted snow would last for months, if there was not too
much ice motion, and this helped keep the sprawling party on
the same course.

They passed beyond the ice foot where the rafted floes were
pressured by the tides, and the going became a bit easier. Still, on
that first day, two wrecked sledges were met returning from the
advance party. The upstanders had been ripped off and one side
of one sledge split from stem to stern. In such cold weather the
wood was extremely brittle and to have two casualties on the first
day was disturbing. They were close enough to shore to obtain
replacements from the base at Cape Columbia, but after this
the wrecked sledges would either have to be repaired by Henson
or abandoned.

The main party covered ten miles on the first march, then
made camp and built their igloos. Each sub-party leader slept
in an igloo with the Eskimos under his command. The Eskimos
were nervous, seeing bad omens in practically everything that
happened. MacMillan had trouble with his men that first night.
He wrote of it:

Our snow igd-loos were up in an hour. The dogs were given
their one pound of frozen pemmican each, and were sound asleep in
a few minutes, round balls of fur in the snow, with their bushy tails
a coverlet for eyes and nose. A few deft strokes of the snow knife
fashioned a door for the entrance, and this was sealed with loose
snow as tightly as any block in the structure. A peephole over the
door to watch the dogs and a four-inch ventilation hole in the roof
completed our shelter.

Six ounces of alcohol were poured into the aluminum cup of our
stove but it refused to burn. A lighted match went out as if it had
been put into a cup of water. The Eskimos were plainly worried. It
always did burn, why not now? An evil spirit must be in the igd-loo.
Immediately Commander [Peary] dispelled all fears by tearing up
bits of paper and placing them upon the surface of the alcohol which
refused to evaporate in such low temperature. The heat from the

burning paper completed the work, and in nine minutes we had hot tea.[42]

This was but a foretaste of the effects of intense cold. During the days to come the few bottles of medicinal whisky froze solid, kerosene froze into a mush, and condensed milk became brittle as rock candy. Frostbite appeared on noses and cheeks as black patches; the tips of fingers became horny, cracked, and bleeding. And since it caused excruciating pain to breathe in the frozen air through the tender passages of the nose, all the men had to breathe through their mouths. This caused the condensation of breath around the face. The moisture then froze the hood of the kooleth until it sometimes became impossible for a man to turn his head.

As they began the second day's march they saw ahead ominous clouds marking the presence of open water. Soon they came to a lead a quarter-mile wide, and it had opened since the advance party had passed. There was nothing to do but make camp and wait for the lead to freeze over or close.

At this moment some of the men wondered why a boat had not been provided for such an emergency. Peary had carefully considered this but decided it was impractical. There were twenty-two men, nineteen sledges, and 133 dogs, plus five tons of supplies and equipment—no job for a canvas boat. By the time a substantial craft was loaded, the lead might close. Also, such a boat would be a mass of ice in one crossing and useless thereafter. In comparatively warm temperatures farther south the Eskimos sometimes placed inflated sealskins under their sledges, thus converting them into crude boats for small leads. Though Peary had several such floats with him, he knew that such a method would be impractical in these northern temperatures of forty and fifty degrees below zero. A sealskin dipped into these waters would become a sheet of metal, and could never again be refolded or packed without breaking. There was no practical solution to the crossing of an open lead save that of waiting for it to freeze over or to close.

During that night the air was suddenly filled with crashing

and screaming, which meant the shores of the lead were being pressed together. They broke camp and crossed over, but now there was no sign of the trail made by Borup's and Bartlett's advance parties. When the lead closed, the northern ice had shifted a mile and a half, and it required extensive lateral exploration to find the trail and continue north.

A few hours' march and they discovered a trail *returning*, headed toward land! These marks had been made by Borup's sub-party, who had come south to make contact with the main party but missed it in the shifting ice. Borup had gone on to the shore base to pick up additional supplies of the vitally needed alcohol. Peary immediately dispatched Marvin and old Kyotah, an expert trail-finder, back to shore to find Borup and bring him forward to the main party.

During that night the main party made Bartlett's third advance station and occupied his abandoned igloos. They watched with great concern as the thermometers began to rise. During that night the temperature rose from fifty degrees below zero to only nine degrees below. This was bad news, indeed, for it meant more open water. And they hadn't even yet come to the Big Lead, the principal barrier between them and the floating ice cap on which rode the North Pole.

After a brief sleep, the expedition roused itself, had breakfast, harnessed up the dogs, and pushed on. Within an hour they came upon Bartlett and his Eskimos. They had built their igloo and were camped beside a vast expanse of water, the Big Lead. It was one hundred yards wide and extended to the east and west as far as the eye could see. The water was black and restless. To fall into it meant death.

Bartlett greeted them dolefully. "I've been here twenty-four hours."

Peary nodded. "We expected some hold-up at the Big Lead."

"It'll never freeze over in this weather," Bartlett said.

"Then we'll have to wait for it to close."

"Commander, it's wider today than it was yesterday, by God!"

"It'll close," Peary said firmly. "Or freeze. We'll get across it."

In his determined optimism Peary did not mention the fact that time was of the essence. They could certainly get across going north, but if it was too late in the season, the summer sun might well prevent their recrossing it on the way home.

They made camp and the south shore of the Big Lead was dotted with igloos and sledges and dogs and impatient men. They waited the next day, and the next, and the next. The morale of the Eskimos began to sink. They stared across the open water at the distant ice cap and more and more it looked like the Abode of Evil Spirits. And even if they did cross this water they might never return. They might never again see their wives and children.

Henson encouraged them and bolstered them the best he could, but there came a time when his words were helpless against the facts. The Eskimos demanded to know why the Big Lead remained open. It could only be because of the spirits' anger at their invasion. Any man could see that. Even Pearyaksoah understood it, for see how he frowned and paced alone. He obviously knew that his magic was not strong enough to force the waters to close.

The inaction was indeed getting on Peary's nerves. In writing of this, Peary revealed pessimism for the first time: "Only one who has been in a similar position could understand the gnawing torment of those days of forced inaction, as I paced the floe in front of the igloos most of the time, climbing every little while to the top of the ice pinnacle back of the igloos to strain my eyes through the dim light. . . ."[43]

After four days Henson saw panic building among his Eskimo friends and he took the problem, not to the preoccupied commander, but to MacMillan. This young teacher had developed into a resourceful trail man and had Peary's confidence. Henson explained to him that if something wasn't done to divert the Eskimos there was a chance of mass desertion and a break for shore.

MacMillan thought about the problem for a moment, then asked, "Do the Eskimos have any contests? Any athletics?"

"There's a fingerpull, and a wristpull, and wrestling," Matt said.

"Good! We'll add a tug of war, sprints, jumps, relays, weight lifting! We'll have our own field day and our own Arctic Olympics. Tell the men there will be prizes for the champions and a chance for all to prove their mettle!"

It turned into a great day with excitement running high. Sprints were a little difficult in the heavy clothing, and complicated by the fact that the noncompetitive Eskimos couldn't seem to get the idea they were to run *against* each other, beat the other man over the finish line. Still, the prizes were proudly received and, more important, all thought of the open water, the malevolent Styx, was banished.

The excitement of the games occupied the Eskimos for two days, and then the old fears began to creep back among them. March 9, 10, and 11 were days of waiting and watching. Precious time was disappearing, food was being eaten, fuel consumed, and the distance to the Pole was being shortened by not a single yard.

A pressing new problem was intensified by this delay: Borup and Marvin had not arrived. They were bringing new supplies of fuel that Peary considered essential to the expedition, especially since the long wait here at the Big Lead, and each day he scanned the horizon to the south for some sign of them. But there was none.

Dissatisfaction among the Eskimos reached a new peak, and this time Peary took a hand, calling Henson to his igloo for consultation. "There are always some ringleaders in this kind of thing, Matt," he said. "Who talks most against going on? Who is most fearful and disloyal? Who infects the others?"

"Pooadloona is the worst," Henson said. "He is a quitter and a whiner. There is no way I can talk to him."

"And who else?"

"Panikpa."

"I am going to banish them," Peary said. "I'll give them the poorest dogs and enough food and send them home without any presents of weapons or wood. They will not be allowed to stay aboard the *Roosevelt* but must walk all the way back to their village at Etah. That will stiffen the rest of the Eskimos."

Henson could think of no good argument against this step, and it reacted upon the rest of the men just as Peary had predicted. As the two lonely figures hitched up their dogs and drove away in the mysterious half-light of the Polar ice cap, their friends watched them go with sober eyes. There were no complaints that night.

For the past two days the temperature had been going down. On March 11 the day was clear and calm and forty degrees below zero. The Big Lead was frozen over. Peary gave orders to strike camp. In his igloo he left a note for Marvin and Borup. It read:

Have waited here [6] days. Can wait no longer. We are short of fuel. Push on with all possible speed to overtake us. Shall leave note at each camp. When near us rush light sledge and note of information about to overhaul us. Expect send back Dr. & Eskimos 3 to 5 marches from here. He should meet you & give you information. We go straight across this lead (E.S.E.). There has been no lateral motion of the ice during 7 days. Only open and shut. *Do not camp here.* CROSS THE LEAD. Feed full rations & speed your dogs. It is *vital* you overtake us and give us fuel. Leaving at 9 a.m. Thursday, Mar. 11. PEARY. P.S. On possibility you arrive too late to follow us, have asked captain take general material from your bags.[44]

On March 12 MacMillan was sent forward to break trail and now it was his turn to face the difficulties of navigation. The simple process of using a compass was complicated by the fact that they were north of the Magnetic North Pole. Also, the Magnetic Pole is not constant, but undergoes yearly geographical changes. Generally it is in the area of Canada's Boothia Peninsula and Prince of Wales Land, fluctuating between 70 and 74 degrees north latitude. When the expedition left land at Cape Columbia it was about 787 miles north of the Magnetic North Pole, and they got farther from it each day. MacMillan was working with a compass that pointed various degrees of southward!

Moreover, it was not entirely accurate even in its designation of the shifting Magnetic Pole. There is a degree of error in all needles, depending in large measure on geographical location. Accurate navigation is possible only when the variation between what the needle points and true north is known. Now, on March 12 in the Arctic ice cap, MacMillan calculated that the westerly variation of his compass was 112 degrees.

MacMillan wrote of that day:

To keep a fairly accurate course toward the Pole, it was our custom to place the compass in the snow, well away from any local attraction such as metal on sledges or equipment, and sight due north allowing for a westerly variation of the compass of one hundred and twelve degrees. We then worked for several hours toward the most conspicuous landmark, such as a peculiarly shaped knob of ice which happened to be on the course.

On reaching our objective, the compass was then resorted to for a new course. No astronomical observations for latitude and longitude were taken for the simple reason that up to this time the sun had reached the altitude of only about one degree and a half above the horizon. Under such conditions accurate observations are impossible and absolutely useless.[45]

Two marches behind the main party, Borup and Marvin came to the Big Lead and found the commander's note. They asked for a volunteer among their Eskimos to sledge forward and notify Peary that they were about to cross the Big Lead and were bringing the alcohol. Seegloo volunteered and made two forced marches, the second one of eighteen hours. Then, after sleeping but four hours, made another double march to catch the main party and tell them the news. Seegloo made a classic record of trail travel, and as a result of this he was one of the four Eskimos ultimately chosen by Peary to accompany him on the final dash to the Pole.

By the time the party was reunited, they had been on the trail for half a month, and the hardships were beginning to tell, on both dogs and men. Breaking trail was particularly hard, and even so stout and courageous a man as Bob Bartlett had to be withdrawn from time to time. MacMillan, who broke trail with him for several marches, wrote: ". . . I saw so strong a man as Bob Bartlett break down and want his mother as we shivered and shook together on a snow bed in the Far North, his underclothing wringing wet, his clothing a mass of ice, his face scarred with frost, his fingers hard, horny and cracked, his body chafed to sores by walking, plodding endlessly on. . . ."[46]

The almost incredible thing was that under these conditions no man wanted to turn back (except some of the Eskimos). They all knew that only one of them could go the final distance with Peary, and every man wanted to be that one. And failing to be the final one, every man wanted to be allowed to go as far north as possible. They were all completely dedicated, not only to Peary, but to the project, to the conquest.

Since the note left for Borup and Marvin, everyone knew that Dr. Goodsell would be the first sent back. Nor was there any surprise at this. Goodsell, a ponderous man, was the least effective on the trail and, being a doctor, the one most needed back aboard ship with the crew.

On March 14 a sounding was made and the bottom found at 825 fathoms. This meant that the edge of the continental shelf had been left far behind and it was time to reduce the number of mouths to be fed. At this point Goodsell was directed to return to shore. But now something unforeseen happened, a development that was to upset the sledging schedules and be a personal blow to Peary. It concerned MacMillan.

As had become custom on the expedition, the problem was brought to Henson for an opinion before being presented to Peary. Henson was in his igloo with his Eskimos, preparing to bed down, when MacMillan crawled through the entrance and sat for a moment beside the small stove, warming his hands on the cylinder. Henson could see that his guest was disturbed, but he asked no questions. He let MacMillan take his own time. There was some small talk, discussion of the trail, of the dogs, the Eskimos. Then suddenly MacMillan pulled off his kamik and then his sheepskin stocking.

"Matt, I want you to look at my foot," he said.

Henson knelt down and took the foot in his hands, held it up to the flickering light from the stove. Then he looked at Mac-Millan's worried face. "How long has it been like this?" he asked.

"Ever since I got to Cape Columbia," MacMillan said. "The other one is frozen, too. But I can do my work. I've done it this far, haven't I?"

"Yes, but the time may come when you can't."

"You think I should show them to the commander?"

"Absolutely," Henson said.

MacMillan put his kamik back on, left Henson's igloo, and walked the few yards to Peary's. When the commander took one look at the foot he said, "You'll return to the ship at once and get those feet taken care of."

He did not say a word about his disappointment. He had come to depend greatly on MacMillan, had planned to take him far north, perhaps even all the way. They walked out on the trail together, then Peary grasped MacMillan warmly by the hand and said, "If I am not back by the first of June, tell Mr. Gushue [first mate] to get the ship ready and go home. And, MacMillan, if you can possibly do it, sledge westward to Ward Hunt Island and place there a cache of food. Also lay down caches of food on the North Greenland shore. We may land there starving, as we did on the last trip."

On March 14 Goodsell with two Eskimos, one sledge, and twelve dogs turned south. On March 15 MacMillan with two sledges, two Eskimos, and fourteen dogs turned south. Borup, Marvin, Bartlett, Henson, and Peary continued north. Henson went ahead to break trail.

Late in the afternoon of the 15th there came loud reports and rumblings from the north. This could only mean that leads were opening up ahead. When they came to open water they made it across by loading the dogs and sledges onto large ice cakes and ferrying them across. Borup's team started to slip into the water but he grabbed the traces and pulled them to safety, saving the precious supplies on the sledge.

At the end of five marches it was time to send back another supporting party. Peary chose Borup. This was a big disappointment to the young man, but he recognized that he was the least experienced of the men left, and he took the decision with a show of good humor. He had hoped to go farther, but said he was grateful to be allowed to go this far. He was at 85 degrees, 23 minutes north latitude.

With three Eskimos and sixteen of the poorest dogs, he headed back toward shore. He later wrote: "I knew that from now on the Eskimos would need no urging to travel long and sleep little and hustle all the time."[47] Borup's party made land at Cape Columbia in seven marches, as against eleven outward ones.

The remaining units were now reorganized, each unit being made up of three men instead of four. It was now continuous daylight and the trail-breaking party could start out twelve hours ahead of the main body, each morning abandoning its igloos for the oncoming men. Having a ready-made igloo waiting at the end of a day's march was a great boon to the men of the main party. Of course, it was a double burden on the trail-makers. This job was rotated between Marvin, Bartlett, and Henson. Peary always came up in the rear, not only to keep effective command and see that no Eskimos fled, but also to save himself for the final effort at the Pole.

On March 23 the camp was past the 86th parallel, 200 miles from land. On March 26 they were at 86 degrees, 38 minutes, and it was time to send another supporting party back. Henson confided in his diary that he expected to receive the order, but it was given to Marvin. With two Eskimos, one sledge, and seventeen dogs he turned south with Peary's final warning in his ears: "Be careful of the leads, my boy."

Marvin survived the leads, but not his companions. On April 10, just a few marches from shore, he was murdered by one of the Eskimos. There had been a quarrel over rations and whether or not the younger Eskimo boy was to be allowed to ride on the sledge. He claimed to be very tired, but Marvin refused permission. Thereupon, the older Eskimo, a cousin, took up the quarrel with Marvin, finally grabbing a gun and shooting him in the head. Marvin's body was thrown into the water of the first open lead.

Since murder is an adjunct of civilization and almost unknown among the Eskimos, this act revealed the great pressures under which these simple people were being placed.

When the Eskimos first returned to the *Roosevelt* they reported merely that Marvin had slipped and drowned. It was not until years later, when the murderer was baptized a Christian, that he confessed.

The expedition had now been reduced to three parties: Henson's, Bartlett's, and Peary's. They had superior dogs and increased rations and steadily improving ice conditions. True, the wind continued to be in the northerly quadrants, not pleasant to face, but they traveled fast, with five marches averaging 15.8 nautical miles. On March 28 they passed Peary's 1906 record, 87 degrees, 6 minutes north latitude. If nothing else, they were now the farthest north of any men in the history of civilization. But that was not enough . . . for any of them. And the great, unspoken question that loomed was who would be ordered to turn back next. Would it be Bartlett or Henson? This would be the final turn-back; the remaining man would share Peary's destiny.

On the night of March 29 they faced a wide lead and made camp. Bartlett took a sounding and found no bottom at 1,260 fathoms. Leads suddenly opened between their igloos and the party was threatened with separation and perhaps even drowning. But the weather turned mercifully cold, thirty degrees below zero, with a bitter northwest breeze. The lead froze over and they were able to advance, but over ice so thin that it buckled beneath their sledges as they raced full speed across it.

April 1 would see the completion of five marches since Marvin's turn-back; it would be the cut-off point for the last supporting party. Peary now had to choose the man to continue with him. He told Bartlett to prepare to return to shore. Henson was to continue.

Strangely, no one seemed surprised or disappointed. Bartlett had just about worn himself out, for he had broken trail most of the time. He had one request, that he be allowed to make a short forced march north by himself in the hope of passing the 88th parallel. This was granted, and when he returned to camp he took an observation and found the camp was at 87 degrees, 46 minutes, 49 seconds. He now knew he had failed to make the 88th, but he had been farther north than any other human being on record.

Now two Eskimos and the poorer dogs, eighteen of them, were sorted out for Bartlett's return. Four Eskimos were to go on north with Peary and Henson. They were Ootah, Ooqueah, Seegloo, and Egingwah.

The farewells were almost casual. "Good-by, Captain," Peary said. "Take care of yourself. Clean up the ship when you get back. Don't worry about me. I'll be back."

Bartlett tried to thank him for the honor of coming this far, but he turned inarticulate. Peary broke in, "It's all in the game. And you've been at it long enough to know how hard a game it is."

Bartlett nodded and said, "Good-by, sir."

Henson was waiting for Bartlett by his sledge and when the bluff and grizzled sea captain came up to him there was a moment of speechless emotion.

"The commander is tired," Bartlett finally said.

"We're all tired," Matt said with a grin.

"God, yes," Bartlett said with feeling. After another moment of silence, "Take care of him, Matt."

"We'll take care of each other. Like always."

"How long you two been searching for the goddamn Pole?"

"Eighteen years."

Bartlett shook his head. "Eighteen years!" He thrust out his hand. "This time you gotta make it, Matt."

Henson agreed. "This time we gotta."

Bartlett waved his hand, then became part of a small caravan south. It grew smaller and smaller and finally disappeared.

Peary and Henson stood alone. After eighteen years in the North and dozens of companions they again stood alone. They were 132 miles from the North Pole. They stood at the precipice of their lives. Within a matter of days they would be heroes or they would be dead.

What had driven them to the point of this awful choice? Or rather, to the point of no choice at all? In some future leisure, if there was to be any, they might be able to count the spurs that gouged their flesh, but not now. Now their bodies were living pain, giving no room for contemplation, or for any thought. They were now automatons whose springs had been wound and whose courses had been set at some earlier time.

They were capable only of marching northward as long as they could walk, and failing that, they would crawl, and failing their goal, they would die. If they were not insane, there was in them a lack of sanity.

[XIX]

They planned to reach the Pole in five marches. How many marches had they made in their twenty-two years together? Two thousand? Four thousand? They didn't know. But five more marches seemed now so very few. Surely, nothing could prevent them from reaching the Pole.

At midnight on April 2 Henson left camp with his team to break trail. Following him came Ootah, then the main party with Peary. Henson marched for ten hours, then made camp and with Ootah built the igloos for the overtaking party. They had covered thirty miles.

They took only a few hours' sleep and were off again on the morning of April 3. The weather was clear and calm. They covered twenty miles and made camp.

Again they took only the minimum sleep, and shortly after midnight on April 4 they were again moving forward. There was one disturbing development: the temperature kept rising. Also, the tides of the approaching full moon were at work. The opening of major leads was to be expected at any moment. In fact, the entire Polar cap might become fragmented, and this gave urgency to their marches. That they might be trapped by open waters and never be able to return south to shore was not what quickened them, but the fear that they might be cut off from their prize to the north.

With the reduction of loads through the consumption of food and fuel, they were able to press on with the illusion of greater speed. Actually, their own exhaustion was such that they were just able to keep the pace.

On the evening of April 4 Peary took a sight with the sextant. It was a long and difficult operation, particularly because of the condition of his eyes. Both he and Henson were suffering from snow-blindness, and the ulcerated condition of his eyeballs made it torture to remove the heavily smoked glasses and look with naked eyes into the instrument. After a long and careful look and figuring with pencil and paper, he said, "We're at 89 degrees."

They were one degree from the Pole! Sixty miles away was the prize.

They started north, driving the dogs at a trot. On the night of April 5 they found themselves completely played out and had to camp for sleep. When they awoke, observation showed them at 89 degrees, 25 minutes, which meant they were thirty-five miles from the Pole. They could make it in a single march, with any luck. Surely they had earned some luck.

The next march was begun before midnight of April 5. The sky was overcast. Very little snow lay upon the ice, so little that it had been difficult to make igloos at this camp. The air temperature had risen to fifteen degrees below zero, which lessened the friction of the sledge runners on the ice but increased the danger of leads.

Henson went forward to break trail. After a run of what he estimated to be fifteen miles, he held up for Peary and the Eskimos to join him and they had tea. They now believed themselves ten miles short of the Pole. A final march! Henson snapped his long whip above the ear of his king dog, cried "Huk!" and the sledge moved forward with the sibilance of steel on ice, a sound that seemed to have been in his ears for a lifetime. Ootah moved his sledge in behind. Ooqueah, Seegloo, Egingwah, and Peary prepared to follow.

Henson trotted beside his sledge, feeling a mounting excitement. His exhaustion, his frozen flesh, his lacerated eyeballs were all forgotten in the drama of each yard gained. In this fever of the final chase he also lost some of his judgment. There could be no other explanation of what now happened.

He came to the edge of a lead that had only recently frozen over with young ice. His team drew up and waited for his order. Normally he would have scouted to east or west to find firmer ice, but he could not endure the thought of such delay. He viewed the young ice and decided it would hold. "Huk!" he cried, and snapped the whip.

A few yards onto the ice and it was clear they were in trouble. The thin sheet began to bend, to undulate beneath their weight. The dogs crouched to their bellies and whimpered, but Henson refused to turn back. "Huk!" he cried. And as they advanced he walked spread-legged to distribute his weight.

A new, cutting sound came to his ears and he looked down to see that the sledge runners were cutting through the bending sheet of ice and throwing up a wet wake of bubbles. He cried out frantically to the dogs and threw his weight against the sledge in an effort to get it on firm ice. But this pressure was fatal, for it broke the ice beneath his feet and he went down. For a moment his furs were buoyant and waterproof, then he felt the searing pain of the water pouring into his boots. He began striking out, clutching for something solid, but the thin ice broke beneath his flailing arms and the pain came higher and higher on his body.

He was filled with a wild anger against the fate that had brought him within a few miles of the Pole, only then to destroy him. Still pain crept upward, and there was nothing he could do.

Suddenly his descent was checked; then, by some miracle, he began to rise in the water. He felt himself being lifted clear of the water and dropped down on firm ice, like a beached fish. He looked up into the brown and stolid face of Ootah who still gripped him by the back of his kooletah.

Without a word the Eskimo went efficiently about the work to be done. He tethered the dogs, pulled off Matt's boots to put his feet against his own warm, dry belly, and then began methodically to beat the ice out of Matt's bearskin pants. When the feet were warm, he got dry boots from the sledge and helped Matt into them.

There was no way Matt could thank his friend for saving his life; this was a normal and almost routine act on the trail. He smiled at the Eskimo and said, "Ootah is very strong."

Ootah frowned, disdainful of such flattery. He said, "Ootah not piblokto like Miy Paluk. Ootah not go out on young ice."

Henson accepted the deserved rebuke and busied himself untangling the trace on his team. The main party had now caught up with them, and it was discovered that Peary, too, had gone through the ice, though not so badly. He had changed his kamiks and was striding quickly to keep the circulation going in his feet.

Peary led the combined party a few miles north, then called a halt. He said to Henson in a matter-of-fact voice, "Matt, this may be it. We'll take an observation."

There was a wind blowing and Henson knew what had to be done. With his snow knife he built a snow windshield. Then he took the instrument box and bedded it firmly in the snow leeward of the shield. He threw down a fur skin, partly to protect Peary's eyes during the observation and partly to keep the snow from melting by body heat and thus unsettling the instrument box.

Their latitude would be determined by the altitude of the sun above the visible horizon as measured by a sextant. However, there was no horizon this day. Gray sky blended into gray ice without anything to mark where one or the other ended. It was, therefore, necessary for Peary to make an artificial horizon.

He placed a small wooden trough on top of the level instrument box and filled it with mercury that had been carried next to his body to keep it fluid. Then he covered the trough with two panes of glass, placed like a tent, to prevent any air currents from rippling the surface of the mercury and distorting the sun's reflection. Removing his dark glasses, painfully blinking his inflamed eyes, he lay down on the rug and grasped the sextant firmly in his hands.

By propping himself on his elbows, he was able to look through the eyepiece and into the arrangement of mirrors, then make adjustments to bring the sun's image down until it touched the upper edge of its own reflection in the trough of mercury. Then he sat up to read the degree of arc indicated on the sextant. Using figures he had previously copied out of a nautical almanac and a table of logarithms, he did some rapid calculations.

He looked up at Henson and in a voice flat with exhaustion said, "Eighty-nine degrees and 57 minutes."

They were three miles from the Pole.

The Pole was a concept, a microscopic spot covered by a vast sea of drifting ice. No instrument available to Peary could locate it with final and complete accuracy. The errors inherent in his method meant that he might at this moment be on top of the Pole, or it might be three miles away in any direction. In all practical terms they had reached their goal.

Without another word Peary packed up his instruments. Then he surrendered to his body. He lay down and fell asleep. Henson lay down beside him and he, too, was instantly asleep.

Seegloo, Egingwah, Ooqueah, and Ootah stood about in bewilderment. *This* was the place, the goal, the prize? They had traveled all those tortuous miles for *this?* But it was no different from the sea and the ice and the sky a hundred miles south, or two hundred, or four! What had driven these two sleeping men to spend a lifetime reaching *this* spot? Was there something here their Eskimo eyes did not see? They asked each other these questions and could find no answers. They sensed that they never would understand. They, too, lay down and went to sleep.

When Henson woke up he saw Peary sitting erect but motionless beside him. He remembered where they were, at the North Pole, and he cried out to Peary in sheer exuberance. Peary turned bloodshot eyes toward him and said in a dead voice, "I'll take Egingwah and Seegloo and make more observations."

Something seemed to have gone out of the man. He was on the verge of a physical breakdown, but it was more than that; the flame that had made him surmount all pain and privation seemed snuffed out. Henson had hoped for a response to his own mood of elation, of victory, but he did not find it then or later. For a time he thought Peary was offended with him and he tried to think back on what he might have done wrong. But he could come up with nothing. Peary had always been taciturn with him, but he had expected *some* demonstration of comradeship or triumph at this climax of their lives. He found its absence simply unaccountable.

He might have understood if he had seen the words Peary put in his diary this day immediately after awaking. They were:

". . . The Pole at last. The prize of three centuries. My dream and goal for twenty years. Mine at last! I cannot bring myself to realize it. It seems all so simple and commonplace."[48]

The attitudes of Peary and the Eskimos were not so very different, after all.

Taking two Eskimos and a double team, Peary made marches in several directions, each time taking observations and entering the result in his journal. At the end of the day he wrote:

. . . I have taken thirteen single, or six and a half double, altitudes of the sun at two different stations, in three different directions, at four different times, and to allow for possible errors in the instruments and observations, have traversed in various directions an area of about eight by ten miles across. At some moment during these marches and countermarches, I had for all practical purposes passed over the point where north and south and east and west blend into one.[49]

Now, at last, Peary was ready for some ceremony. He named their camp "Camp Morris K. Jesup," after the president of the American Museum of Natural History and also of the Peary Arctic Club. Then he said, "Matt, line up the Eskimos for a picture."

From beneath his kooletah he removed the patched and sweat-soaked American flag he had carried for so many years. Then from his sledge he withdrew an amazing collection of other flags, giving one each to Seegloo, Egingwah, Ooqueah, and Ootah. As they lined up before Peary's camera, Henson stood in the middle holding the American flag; flanking him were the Eskimos holding the Delta Kappa Epsilon fraternity flag, the Navy League flag, the Red Cross flag, and the World Ensign of Liberty and Peace, a flag created by the Daughters of the American Revolution.

"Plant the Stars and Stripes over there, Matt," Peary called.

Henson carried the flag to a small mound of ice and drove the staff into the brittle surface. Then Matt instructed the Eskimos to join him in three cheers.

"Hip, hip, hooray," came the straggle of voices with the strange accents. "Hip, hip, hooray," urged on Henson. "Hip, hip, hooray," came the final chorus. The words were caught up by a cutting wind and blown south. Every direction was south.

It was now April 7 and the spring tides were due the last of April. After that, when the leads opened they would not again close, not until fall. And land was over 400 miles away.

To make it home they would have to double-march all the way. This meant starting out in the morning and covering the distance previously made by one march north, then having tea and lunch and covering a second march. Failure to meet this killing schedule by so much as a single march could only increase the grave danger of the trail being destroyed by shifting ice and impassable leads opening between them and land.

Before setting out, Henson saw that all the dogs were double rationed and that all the harnesses and sledges were in good repair. All equipment not vitally necessary to travel was jettisoned. The heavy reel and wire used to make soundings were discarded, thus eliminating a hundred pounds in weight. All they carried was food and fuel, of which they had plenty, and their tools and weapons and clothes. The trail was made; the already constructed igloos waited to shelter them each night. Their only opponent was the warm weather and, of course, their own failing strength.

"We're ready, sir," Henson said to Peary.

The commander nodded and stepped out on the trail to lead them south. He walked bravely alone, while into line behind him fell the five sledges with their drivers walking behind the uprights and crying orders to the dogs.

Peary set a fast pace, as he had to, but within the hour he staggered and almost fell. He righted himself and with supreme effort marched on, but again staggered. Henson ran forward to grab him and hold him upright. The face of his commander, black and crusted from frost and sun, streamed with tears that froze as they ran. His eyes were almost blind and the pain was excruciating. Not only had his eyes given out; his entire body sagged against Henson, all the iron gone out of it. He was an old and sick man.

"Egingwah!" Matt cried. "Bring sledge. Fast!"

When the sledge came up they hurriedly transferred its load to the other sledges, then placed Peary carefully upon it and covered him with furs. In this manner he traveled southward. It was not without protest from the gallant old warrior; each morning he left camp early to walk ahead on the trail, but when the sledges caught up with him, he had expended his small measure of strength and allowed himself to ride.

On April 9, after two days on the trail, a gale descended upon them. Fortunately it was from the north-northeast and to their backs.

The leads were beginning to widen and be more frequent, but as yet they continued to be covered with new ice that could support the lightened sledges and reduced teams. By April 10 the dogs were beginning to show the effect of double marches and several of them were worn out and had to be destroyed. Thirty-five dogs were left, which meant seven to a sledge. On this day they reached the igloos where Bartlett had turned back.

The sun was becoming more dazzling each day and all of them had trouble with their eyes. To take off the goggles would have meant immediate blindness. On April 12 they arrived at the igloos where Marvin had turned back. They were reaching the older and heavier floes, making travel more difficult but safer. The principal worry now was the Big Lead. Would it be open or closed? If they found it open they were doomed.

By April 18 the dogs were almost lifeless from the driving pace and they had to be given a rest and double rations. But land clouds could be seen ahead. The Big Lead was near. The dogs were reduced to thirty.

On April 20, just as they were approaching the Big Lead, Peary came down with the quinsy. He was feverish and his throat ached and he could not sleep. Yet he allowed no stop.

April 21 they came to the Big Lead. It was frozen over. They passed over it and two days later came to blessed land.

The Eskimos went crazy with excitement and jumped and screamed and laughed until they had to sink to the ground and gasp for breath. Henson stood over them and laughed too and cried out, "You see . . . you see now about your devil out there on Ser-mik-suah?"

Ootah nodded and said, "Yes . . . yes. The devil was asleep, or having trouble with his wife, or we should not have come back so easily."

[XX]

Of heroes, Emerson wrote: ". . . he finds a quality in him that is negligent of expense, of health, of life, of danger, of hatred, of reproach, and knows that his will is higher and more excellent than all actual and all possible antagonists."

This had been the quality of Peary's life in the North. And, on a more modest scale, of Henson's. What Peary also had was a sense of history. He knew that the passion in his heart stood for his nation. He, and Henson, could not return from their triumph without some consciousness of their heroism. What they expected in the way of honors was locked in each man's heart, but they had every reason to believe it would be considerable. They were utterly unprepared for the bitter reality that awaited them.

The drama opened slowly, with no one guessing the irony, the excesses that waited in the wings. They arrived at Cape Columbia on April 23, after sixteen marches from the Pole. After two days' rest they pushed on to Cape Sheridan and the *Roosevelt* where they received the tragic news of Marvin's death. The ice released the *Roosevelt* early that summer and they sailed south on July 18, making Etah without incident.

The arrival at this Greenland port was cause for great celebration. The Eskimo tribe welcomed back their relatives, their own

heroes who had gone to the Pole. And this was the time for re-
wards, the passing out of guns and knives and cooking utensils
and whaleboats. But in the midst of all this an amazing bit of
news was brought aboard by Harry Whitney, the sportsman who
had spent the winter hunting there. Whitney said Dr. Frederick
Cook had come through Etah this spring on his way back from
the North and hinted that he had achieved the North Pole.

All the members of the expedition were incredulous, and they
demanded details from Whitney. The hunter was vague, but it
seemed that Cook claimed to have sledged from Cape Thomas
Hubbard to the Pole and back with two Eskimos and two sledges.
Peary pointed out at once that the route was several hundred
miles *longer* than the route taken by Henson and himself, and yet
it was claimed to have been done without supporting parties and
only with the supplies carried on two sledges! Experience of a
lifetime told him this was impossible. He had spent eighteen years
devising the logistics of supplies and supporting parties necessary
to get to the North Pole. It was possible by no other method, he
was convinced.

The entire expedition tried to dismiss the news as nothing more
than Arctic hyperbole. All sorts of fantastic stories could arise
above the Arctic Circle, but once they moved south to the warmer
and saner climates, they generally disappeared. Still, there was
something about the Cook story, or rather about Cook the man,
that promised to cling. The Peary-Cook-Henson destinies had
been intertwined in strange ways ever since that first trip to
Greenland.

There had been respect and even affection between these men
originally. Henson was grateful for the way Cook had cared for
his sun-blinded eyes; Peary was grateful for the skill the doctor
had shown in setting his broken leg; both Peary and Henson had
found the doctor a cheerful companion on the trail and had
hoped to have him with them again.

The break began over Peary's refusal to let Cook lecture about
his experiences with the first North Greenland Expedition; it
deepened as Cook lectured anyway and with florid detail that

Peary considered most unscientific. There continued enough respect on Peary's part to allow Cook to give him a physical examination following his terrible four years in Fort Conger. However,
the fact that Cook pronounced Peary as physically unfit for further northern work certainly brought a deep chill to their relationship.

An open break was in the making in 1906, just before Peary
left on his final expedition. Cook announced he had climbed Mt.
McKinley on the south side and presented his claim to the Explorers Club in New York. Peary was president of the club. Experts began at once to question the claim. The south side of the
peak was inaccessible, they said, and the photograph Cook had sent
was not taken at the top, they charged. Peary, in his capacity
as president, sent Cook a telegram inviting him to appear for-
mally before the club and submit proof of his claim. He was
given a month to comply.

Cook blithely ignored the summons, the challenge, and wired
back, "I am off to nail the Explorers Club Flag to the North
Pole." No one took him seriously. It seemed a transparent method
of ducking an ugly situation.

Peary, sailing north on his own final expedition, had dismissed
the problem from his mind. But upon arrival at Etah on his way
north, Peary discovered that Cook had been there before him and
had left a cache of supplies under the supervision of Rudolph
Franke, a member of the crew of the schooner that had brought
Cook north. Franke was in a pitiable condition, sick with scurvy
and half mad with the loneliness of the North. He begged permission to sail back south on the auxiliary ship *Erik,* which Peary
finally granted. Peary gave stern orders that Cook's supplies were
not to be touched, but saved for him when he returned from
wherever he might be.

Then, giving no further thought to Cook, Peary went north to
the Pole.

Now again at Etah, he found he was not yet free of the man
who seemed forever to dog his steps. He could not really believe

that Cook would lay claim to the Pole, and yet the man's past history seemed to make it possible.

On the second afternoon they were in Etah a knock came on Peary's cabin door. "Come in," he called.

Henson stepped in. "Commander, I have some interesting news."

"Yes, what is it, Matt?"

"The two Eskimos who accompanied Cook are in the settlement. I just met them an hour ago."

"Good Lord, let's talk to them."

"Yes, sir, I thought it would be a good idea. Their names are Etookashoo and Ahpellah."

"Bring them aboard, Matt, at once."

"They are aboard. They're in MacMillan's cabin. I thought you ought to be present when we question them."

Peary jumped up and followed Henson to MacMillan's cabin where the two Eskimos were waiting. MacMillan had spread out charts of the North in the hope of being able to trace the exact Cook route as they questioned his two companions. The Eskimos were but boys of sixteen and seventeen years, but they well knew Henson's reputation and addressed him respectfully and affectionately as Miy Paluk.

As he interviewed them, Henson translated their answers and MacMillan carefully marked the charts. Peary hung nervously over their shoulders. Bit by bit the story was pieced together. Cook and six Eskimos had proceeded west to Ellesmere Island, passed north through the Eureka Channel to the northern end of Axel Heiberg Island. From there they had marched out onto the Polar Sea. After a short march they built their igloos and made camp. Four of the Eskimos returned to land and then home, leaving Cook with Etookashoo and Ahpellah.

They slept in that camp for two nights, then Cook took a picture of the igloo with flag flying and said, "Now we'll go home."

They proceeded southward on a line roughly parallel with the western shore of Axel Heiberg Island, finally establishing a winter camp on the northern shore of North Devon. The following May they crossed Smith Sound to Greenland. It was a remarkable trip, new islands were found, and courage and skill were shown, but the march did not extend to the North Pole.

Again and again Henson questioned the Eskimos on the point. How far out on the Polar Sea did they go? Only one march, they insisted. "Miy," Etookashoo said, "we always see land. Always!"

The two boys never altered their story. Some years later MacMillan came north and engaged them to take him over the exact route they had traveled with Cook. It turned out to be as they described it this day aboard the *Roosevelt*.

At last there were no more questions to be asked by Henson, there were no ambiguities; MacMillan had carefully charted the Cook route. The doctor had, at his farthest north, been 500 miles south of the Pole. They all sighed in relief. The sportsman Whitney must have misunderstood Cook. No man would attempt such a wild deception.

During the following weeks Henson led hunting expeditions to supply the Eskimos with meat through the winter; then on August 26 the *Roosevelt* steamed south. They put in at Turnavik on the Labrador coast where coal waited, then steamed south to Indian Harbor where telegraph facilities would allow them to announce their triumph to the world. They arrived on September 6 and Peary sent wires to his wife, to the Peary Arctic Club, to *The New York Times*, and to the Associated Press. This last wire read simply: "Stars and stripes nailed to the Pole."[50]

These out of the way, the expedition and crew members were allowed to send wires to their families. Henson waited in the long and eager line to send his wire to Mrs. Lucy Henson in her Harlem apartment. He promised to come home at once, and to stay!

Back aboard the *Roosevelt* that afternoon, Henson was leaning on the rail to watch idly as the *Fiona*, a British revenue cutter, approached. The small ship came alongside and her captain announced that he had received a message from a man named Cook and he thought it might be of interest to the *Roosevelt*. The message, sent from Lerwick, Shetland Islands, read: "Reached North Pole April 21, 1908. Discovered land far north. Return to Copenhagen by steamer *Hans Egede*. Frederick Cook."[51]

For centuries scientists and geographers had questioned the possibility of man ever reaching the North Pole. Now, within a space of five days, *two* men claimed to have done it. And so the battle was joined. Henson was to be smack in the middle.

Newspaper reporters sailed northward to meet Peary's boat, and eastward to intercept Cook in Denmark. Other explorers were at first reluctant to question Cook's claim for fear it would look like sour grapes, and the reporters were generally too caught up in the public enthusiasm to be searching in their stories. Of all the correspondents in Copenhagen to greet Cook, only two expressed doubts about his story. One of them was Peter Freuchen, himself an explorer, but his paper, the Copenhagen *Politiken*, refused to print his story.

Without hearing the complete facts, Freuchen's attitude was dictated by his knowledge of the two men. He later said (appropriating a woman editor's phrase), "Cook was a liar and a gentleman. Peary was neither."

While the *Roosevelt* was slowly making her way home, Cook was received by the King of Denmark and, on September 7, was awarded the Royal Danish Geographical Society's Gold Medal.

On the following day Peary wired to *The New York Times:*

Do not trouble about Cook's story or attempt to explain any discrepancies in his installments. The affair will settle itself. He has not been to the Pole on April 21, 1908, or at any other time. He has simply handed the public a gold brick. These statements are made advisedly and I have proof of them. When he makes a full statement of his journey over his signature to some geographical society or other reputable body, if that statement contains the claim that he has reached the Pole, I shall be in a position to furnish material that may prove distinctly interesting reading for the public.[52]

Peary's cable was calm, Olympian, and patronizing. And he completely misjudged the mood of the American public.

Over the past twenty-two years Peary had been constantly in the public eye and, though a hero, the public had tired of him. Always he was going north to discover the Pole, and always he returned without quite doing it. Now suddenly, in the person of Dr. Cook, was a brand-new face. More than that, he was a loner. He had no elaborate equipment, no legions of supporting parties, no wealthy men to pay his bills, no powerful statesmen to praise him. He was the little man, the average man, the David who had conquered where Goliath had failed. Moreover, he was undeniably personable. He had the common touch: he liked people and people liked him. They just plain *wanted* to believe he had discovered the Pole.

When Peary cabled that the public had been given a gold brick, that public was offended; it thought its intelligence had been questioned. And when in reply to this harsh statement Cook gently said, "There is glory enough for all," the public cheered his generosity and damned his traducers.

[XXI]

Seldom in the history of the nation had there been such acrimonious public disputation, most of it among men who knew little about the Arctic regions. In fact, the less knowledge about the North, the more violent the partisan tended to be. Popular sympathy was reflected in the prices paid for the explorers' personal stories: Peary received $4,000 from the *Times*, Cook $24,000 from the *Herald*. A Pittsburgh newspaper conducted a popular vote over the question of who had discovered the Pole, and the result was a ten-to-one victory for Cook. Not only was Cook's claim being taken by many people as valid, but Peary's and Henson's claim was considered a lie.

There was also a small but articulate group who were not so much pro-Cook as anti-Peary. Prominent among them was General Greely, who had long smarted under Peary's blunt analysis of his Arctic expedition. When he announced for Cook, he gave an aura of respectability to that movement which it had previously lacked. That he was acting from pique was not understood until some years later when he reversed himself and grudgingly accepted Peary's claim as valid. He could never, of course, undo the harm he had done to Peary at this moment of crisis.

Cook's return to America was a triumph. His supporters in

New York chartered the steamer *Grand Republic* and with a thousand aboard, steamed down the bay to meet his liner and to escort him to his home. A banquet was held in his honor at the Waldorf-Astoria and a thousand cheering men and women packed the grand dining room. Cook immediately entered on a lecture tour that was without parallel in history. Hundreds of thousands of dollars were taken in as the halls were packed with men who cheered and women who wept.

And what of Peary and Henson and MacMillan and Borup and Bartlett and Goodsell? They were a shocked and subdued band of heroes who returned to the most vicious personal attacks. The height of it was, perhaps, on October 2, the Tercentenary of the Hudson River voyage by Robert Fulton's *Clermont*. A great naval parade up the Hudson was scheduled for the event, and before going north, Peary had promised that the *Roosevelt* would participate. Though he guessed it might be painful, Peary thought highly of his own word and he ordered ship and crew and expedition members to be on hand that day.

It was a gala day, with the shores of the Hudson lined with people and the waters alive with small craft. There was a replica of the *Half Moon* and one of the *Clermont*, along with Navy and Coast Guard boats. The craft were to rendezvous at Newburgh and then sail southward past New York City and out to the Narrows.

The moment the *Roosevelt* steamed south down the Hudson she was greeted by boos and catcalls and derisive whistles. Cook supporters in boats pulled alongside to shout abusively. Peary stood on the foredeck, the members of his expedition lined the rails, and at one point impulsive young Borup started to shout back at their harassers, but Peary whirled on him and said sternly, "Be quiet." Then to the rest of the crew and expedition he said, "No man is to answer back. You will stand at your posts and in silence and dignity. Let them shout. It does them more harm than it does us."

Brave words, but not exactly true. The *Roosevelt* was jeered and insulted all the way to Poughkeepsie and back. Peary stood grimly at his post, refusing by motion or word to indicate he heard, but every word cut his flesh. Of all the men aboard the *Roosevelt,* Henson stood the jeers with the greatest fortitude. For, after all, he was a Negro and he had been taunted before.

Following this humiliation, Peary retired to his Eagle Island home off the coast of Maine and refused to allow any receptions in his honor, or to give any lectures, or to see any newspapermen until his claim to the Pole had been examined and declared valid by reputable scientific organizations. This left the field wide open to Dr. Cook, and he made the most of it. And, though Cook had no personal hand in it, Henson was to become the butt of much of the pro-Cook and anti-Peary propaganda.

When Peary retired to his island, the expedition was, of course, disbanded. Bartlett continued to make a living as a merchant captain; the rest of the men had their college degrees and went back to their interrupted careers. But Henson had no degree, no career except that of assistant to Peary. What could he do now?

When he first returned home to his Harlem apartment, Lucy announced she had quit her job at the bank. She was under the impression that he would make a lot of money for helping discover the North Pole, and he had to disillusion her, gently. His small monthly salary of twenty-five dollars had been generally used up. The Peary Arctic Club voted a bonus of $250 to all members of the expedition and he had that money, but it was hardly sufficient to pay their bills for long. He would look for a job, of course, but in the meantime Lucy returned to the employer she had so proudly left and asked for her job back. She was given it.

Matt got a job. It was handyman in a Brooklyn garage. His pay was sixteen dollars a week.

The job was short-lived, for within that week he returned home one evening to find waiting for him in his living room a round, ebullient man smoking a big cigar. Lucy introduced him as Mr. William Brady. He was the famous Broadway producer and promoter.

He came directly to the point of his visit. "Henson, who's telling the truth, Peary or Cook?"

"Commander Peary," Matt replied.

"Cook never came near the Pole?"

"No, sir. I consider Dr. Cook a friend of mine. But the truth is the truth. He never got out of sight of land."

"Then why in hell don't you speak up?" Brady demanded.

Henson smiled. "I do when anybody asks me the question."

"You're not speaking to enough people. I want to put you on the platform, send you on a lecture tour."

"I've never stood up in front of people and talked!" Matt exclaimed, aghast at the prospect.

"You can learn," Brady cried. "Hell's bells! There's Peary up there in Maine sulking and not speaking in his own behalf, letting Cook have the field to himself. You owe it to Peary to defend him . . . and defend yourself. I'll book you into every major town in the country, by God. Do you have any pictures of the North Pole?"

"Yes, sir. I took some snapshots."

"Good. I'll make them into slides. You get a speech together and we'll rehearse it until you're sure of every word. Come down to my office tomorrow and we'll set up the tour."

When Brady left the small apartment, Lucy smiled up at Matt and said, "A public speaker! My, I'll be proud."

Personal tragedy came from this tour—it caused an irreparable break between Henson and Peary. Matt wrote to Peary asking the loan of some of the pictures he had taken in the North and given to his commander. Peary not only refused use of the pictures; he forbade the lecture tour. Though he did not bother to elucidate them, he had two reasons for this order.

First was his long-standing policy prohibiting his men from using their northern experiences for lectures until after he had written his own accounts and made his own lectures. And second, he wanted *no one* to speak at this time of controversy until the scientific societies had cleared his claim. He did not want to run the risk of having his position jeopardized by any random comments made by Henson, or anyone else.

To Henson this seemed an unfair prohibition. Peary had, in all truth, cut him adrift immediately after the Pole. Twenty-two years of service had been disregarded the moment the objective had been obtained. It could be argued that Peary had no responsibility to the former servant, the former assistant, the man who had saved his life, who had contributed mightily to the realization of his life's dream. The job was done and each man could be expected to go his own way. Certainly Henson would not have opposed such an argument. But, on the other hand, he was broke and he had a wife to support and it did seem to him that he had a right to his own pictures, his own memories. He went ahead with the lecture plans.

Peary was deeply offended by this decision. And the aristocratic Mrs. Peary was coldly furious. She had never been able to accept Henson as anything but a servant, and it seemed to her insupportable that a servant should speak when the master said silence.

At the beginning, William Brady had no firm conviction on the controversy—he was merely doing his job—but he ended up with respect and affection for Matt. Years later he wrote in his autobiography:

I tried to land Cook when he reached Copenhagen on his way back. But he knew all about lecture tours and had already got himself booked for a tour before he ever started for the Pole. . . . I also tried to land Peary . . . but [he] didn't even give me the courtesy of an answer. For the third best—and a pretty good third too—I got Matt Henson, the negro who, along with three [*sic*] Eskimos, had accompanied Peary to the Pole itself. . . . As the only negro in the list of Polar heroes, he was certain to attract a lot of attention from the public in general and be a terrific drawing card for his own race in particular. He was an intelligent, good-looking, soft-spoken, modest fellow who, I was sure, would easily ingratiate himself with audiences.[53]

Brady, despite his show-wisdom, his long experience with audiences, was dead wrong!

He booked Matt's first lecture at Middletown, Connecticut,

taking every possible step to make it a gala event. When he and Henson arrived on the train, the mayor was at the station to greet them, and a brass band led them on parade through the town to the lecture hall. Brady wrote, "It has always been my theory—and it had never failed me before—that the combination of a silk hat and a Sousa March will draw a crowd in any city in America for no reason at all. And here I had Hero No. 2 of the biggest story of the year. Yet the inhabitants of Middletown, acting on some mysterious common impulse, snubbed Henson as completely as if his build-up had consisted of merely a sandwich man."[54]

Receipts that afternoon were thirteen dollars and eighty cents. For the evening lecture they climbed to twenty-three dollars.

Brady decided they needed some headlines and the place to get them was New York. He booked Henson into the Hippodrome. He got the headlines, all right.

The Cook supporters, who thought they had intimidated Peary into silence, were furious to learn that one of his men dared speak out. They packed the Hippodrome. Backstage Matt paced nervously, trying to remember his speech. His mind seemed to have gone completely blank. Brady had bought him an English tweed walking suit, and though it was elegantly cut it was of the densest weave and clung to its sweating victim like an instrument of torture. The high stiff collar threatened to garrote him at any moment. In all his years in the North he had never suffered these exquisite tortures of stage fright.

Brady paced beside him, trailing a cloud of cigar smoke and advice. "Just speak out, Matt. Good and loud. You've got a fine speech but they gotta hear it. Shout it to the back row."

"Yes, sir," Matt said miserably.

"And just remember you're a hero! You're braver than any man out there!"

"Oh, Lord!" Henson breathed, half comment and half prayer.

It came time for him to go on the stage. He walked stiffly, as if his legs were brittle, and took his place at the rostrum. The spotlight burned down on his head beaded with perspiration.

"Ah . . .," he said.

There was a silence in the hall, not one of sympathy, but a leering sort of hostility.

"I . . . ah . . .," Matt began again. And again he came to dead center. A whistle came from the balcony and then some catcalls.

Something had to be done to get the lecture going, and Brady did it. He marched out on the stage and took his place beside Henson. Then he looked around challengingly at the audience and boomed, "My man Matthew Henson is here to answer every and all questions. If you have any, speak up!"

A man jumped up in the front row and with practiced lawyer's gestures, he leveled a finger at Henson and demanded, "Were you at the North Pole?"

"Yes, sir," Henson replied promptly, "I was."

"How did you know you were at the North Pole?" the lawyer intoned.

Matt paused a moment, then said, "Well, Commander Peary told me we were."

Derisive laughter swept through the hall. The prosecutor in the front row waited for it to subside, then, mimicking Henson's voice, he repeated, "Commander Peary told you you were." This drew new laughter. Now the lawyer demanded, "Can you take an observation on a sextant?"

"Yes, sir," Henson replied.

"How do you take an observation?" the lawyer thundered.

Matt looked stunned. He *was* stunned. In the heat of the questioning he had claimed too much and trapped himself. He couldn't take an observation at all. As he stood, mute, the audience began to shout and stamp. The roar mounted until there was a full-scale riot. Henson and Brady were led out the rear door by the police.

Now the Cook supporters had their battle cry: Peary had taken an ignorant Negro north with him instead of a scientist so that he could conceal the fact that he hadn't reached the Pole!

Thus the stain of race prejudice was added to the already ugly picture. Southern governors later refused to attend functions honoring Peary.

Henson, who had hoped to help Peary, had ended by harming him. Not that he could have done otherwise, and his taking or not taking to the lecture platform had no bearing on the Cook supporters' determination to smear Peary. What he did do, however, was to give their propaganda a dramatic springboard, a projectile velocity that was to carry it far into the future.

Twenty years later J. Gordon Hayes was to write a hostile biography of Peary in which he said:

He [Peary] was not a scientist, and he seldom took out men who were qualified to conduct the investigations that are the first essential in new countries. If he included a few students in his staff, as he did on two or three of his expeditions, he was careful not to permit them to accompany him to his most distant points; though that is precisely what is wanted, and what the great explorers always do. Peary preferred to have Henson and the Eskimos as his companions, in spite of the fact that all of them, from the most important standpoints, were perfectly useless.[55]

Hayes and the other Cook supporters missed the *essential* of the Polar trip. It was survival! Peary was perfectly capable of taking celestial and solar observations, but he needed Henson and the Eskimos to get him to the Pole and back again. Without them he could never have made it.

The members of the expedition, without exception, rallied to Henson's defense. Bartlett wrote: ". . . I don't deny that it would have been a great thrill to have stood at the peak of our globe. But don't forget that Henson was a better dog driver than I. So I think Peary's reasoning was sound."[56]

George Borup wrote: ". . . Matt Henson, a jack-of-all-trades, and differing from that person in being apparently a master of them all; a dandy sledge-maker, good shot, and as good a dog driver as the best Eskimos. Many have been the criticisms of the commander for having taken Matt with him in the final dash, but we who knew his merits felt that Matt, from his long training in the North, thoroughly deserved to go."[57]

Donald MacMillan, the most thoughtful man in the expedition, wrote:

One question I have been asked again and again . . . is, "Why did Peary select a colored man to accompany him to the Pole rather than one of his white assistants?"

Matthew Henson first went north with Peary in 1891. He was with him on his long trip over the Greenland Ice Cap in 1893. He was with him when he rounded the northern end of Greenland in 1900. He was with him off Cape Hecla in 1902. He was with him when he broke the world's record in 1906. He was the most popular man aboard the ship with the Eskimos. He could talk their language like a native. He made all the sledges which went to the Pole. He made all the stoves. Henson, the colored man, went to the Pole with Peary because he was a better man than any of his white assistants. . . . After his many failures, Commander Peary owed it to himself, his family, his loyal backers, his country, to take the most effective man, to use the most serviceable. And this he did. And he won![58]

But these reasoned words could not be heard in the gales of prejudice that swept about Henson and Peary. Few people came to Henson's lectures because few people wanted the truth if it meant giving up their passions. Brady canceled the tour and Henson returned home with a couple of hundred dollars to show for all the effort and pain.

Peary was not without his supporters, but they were less boisterous than the Cook men and therefore seemed even fewer in number than they were. But slowly the reputable societies began to react. The Explorers Club dropped Cook from membership after hearing testimony of fraud on his Mt. McKinley claim. The Arctic Club dropped him two days later. On January 4, 1910 the Council of the Brooklyn Institute of Arts and Sciences expelled him from membership.

All these months the University of Copenhagen had been demanding Cook's documentary proof of his North Pole claim, and all these months he had said they were in the possession of Harry Whitney. But when this sportsman finally returned to America, he denied ever having received any documents from Cook. The doctor blandly said that it was quite all right because he had duplicates. Under the greatest pressure, he finally sent these "duplicates" to Denmark.

The Consistory of the University of Copenhagen, after seeing the documents, reported on January 19, 1910: ". . . The Committee is therefore of the opinion that the material sent us for investigation can furnish no proof whatsoever that Dr. Cook has reached the North Pole."[59] Privately, members of the Committee were more outspoken. Commander Gustav Holm said, "We examined Cook's observations . . . and agreed unanimously that they were worthless."[60] Dr. Knud Rasmussen, a member of the Committee who had originally been a Cook supporter, said, "When I saw the observations, I realized it was a scandal . . . the papers which Cook sent to Copenhagen are most impudent. . . ."[61]

One by one the scientific societies closed their doors to Cook, and in 1910 he disappeared, going to South America to live. But the air he left behind had been poisoned against Peary and Henson.

[XXII]

During the next two years Peary fought bitterly for his reputation, for his claim to the Pole, and for retirement from the Navy on a Rear Admiral's pension. He was subject to the most hostile examination by some pro-Cook senators, and harassed by the line Navy brass who had long been jealous of the fame showered upon a reserve officer.

In the midst of this travail there came a letter from Henson. It was dated April 10, 1911, and it read:

Dear Sir:

I am writing to ask a favor of you which I sincerely hope will be granted. My wife and I are writing a book and would like very much to have you write a preface. I could think of no better person than yourself, as the best portion of my life has been spent in your service and I have tried to the best of my ability to serve you faithfully. I can assure you wherever your name has been mentioned in the book it has been in the most glowing terms. Thanking you in advance for a reply, I am,

> Yours very truly,
> Matthew A. Henson[62]

Peary did not reply for two weeks and when he did, the salutation on the letter read "Dear Sir."[63] To call Henson "Sir" was a

rebuke, of course. Yet, having done that, Peary went on to perform an act of justice, even generosity. He not only agreed to
write a foreword, after reading the manuscript, but directed
Henson to take the book to his own publisher, Frederick A. Stokes
Company.

On July 29, 1911 Peary received a letter from Stokes which
read:

Thank you very much for your telegram regarding the Henson
book. I have written him, asking him to call, and I hope to arrange
matters at once. Of course, his ideas of terms may be prohibitive, but
I will do my best. . . . In general, it seems to me best not to attempt
to polish the work much, but merely to omit anything that is too
strong. I think that the book will be much more interesting if left as
nearly as possible in the form in which Henson wrote it, with all its
defects, as to revise this away would be to destroy the straight-
forwardness, sincerity and personality shown. . . .[64]

The book, entitled *A Negro Explorer at the North Pole*, was
published by Stokes in February, 1912. The foreword was Peary
at his best, blunt and just. He wrote: ". . . The example and
experience of Matthew Henson, who has been a member of each
and all of my Arctic expeditions since '91 . . . is only another
one of the multiplying illustrations of the fact that race, or color,
or bringing-up, or environment count nothing against a determined heart, if it is backed and aided by intelligence."[65]

Far from avoiding the race question, Peary met it head-on. By
this courageous foreword he did much to heal the wounds he and
Henson had inflicted on each other. However, for the rest of their
lives they remained slightly estranged, partly because of the world
in which they lived. In the northern wilderness they were bound
together by the nature of the life; in civilization they were separated by the nature of the life.

Henson's book, as his lectures, died quickly. The difference was
that the book's short life was not spent amid shouted abuses,
smears, and jeers. It died quietly. Which was even sadder.

Meantime, Peary was winning his fight for recognition. Over

the objections of many line officers, he was promoted to Rear Admiral in the Navy and then retired on a pension close to $8,000 a year. After long and acrimonious hearings, the House Committee on Naval Affairs reported out, and the Congress passed, an official thanks. It read:

"The Senate and House of Representatives of the United States of America, in Congress assembled. That the thanks of Congress be, and the same are hereby, tendered to Robert E. Peary, United States Navy, for his Arctic explorations, resulting in reaching the North Pole. Approved March 4, 1911. (signed) Wm. Howard Taft, President of the United States."[66]

What was notable in the resolution, aside from the awkwardness, was the phrase, "reaching the North Pole." The Congress sidestepped the whole issue of who reached it first, who discovered it.

The world's scientific societies were not so mealymouthed; they came out in unequivocal support of Peary's claims. The National Geographic Society was first to honor him with a gold medal, and this was followed by honors from the Royal Geographical Society in London and then from almost every major society around the world. The medals and scrolls became so numerous that Peary had special display cases constructed to hold them. His recognition had been tragically delayed, but now it came in abundance.

To be sure, none of the scrolls mentioned Henson; none of the medals carried his profile; no banquet was held in his honor. The avalanche of praise for Peary buried the assistant. Except for his old comrades of the North and a few Negro friends, he was forgotten.

Charles Anderson was one of the few who did not forget. He was a Negro but also a politician of some skill and influence. One day he said to Henson, "Matt, you still working in that Brooklyn garage?"

"Sure am. Why?"

"Damn it, man, you deserve a better job than that. You deserve a job of respect and dignity."

"Fine," Matt grinned. "You got one for me?"

"Well, no. But the country owes you something. If Peary can be retired as a Rear Admiral and get the thanks of Congress, you ought to get something."

"Peary deserved everything he got, Charlie. And you know how a lot of people feel about me going to the Pole instead of Bartlett, or some other white man. I don't want to stir things up again."

"You may not want to stir things, but *I'm* sure as hell going to. I've got some influence in Washington and I'm going to see the government does something for you."

Several months passed and Matt and Lucy forgot about the conversation. Then one night Charlie Anderson appeared at their door, a grin of triumph splitting his face. "Congratulations, Matt," he cried. "Your appointment came through from Washington."

"What appointment?" Matt and Lucy chorused.

"Signed by President Taft himself!" Charlie crowed.

"*What* was signed by President Taft?"

"You've got a job, Matt. You go to work at the Customs House, the United States Customs House downtown."

"Is that a fact?" Matt said with a grin. Lucy took his arm proudly. "What kind of a job is it?"

"Well." Suddenly Charlie Anderson seemed deflated. He sat down and took out his handkerchief and blew his nose. "Well . . . it was the only thing available, Matt."

"Okay, what kind of a job?"

"You're a messenger boy."

The job paid $900 a year. Later the salary was increased to $2,000. During the Christmas holidays Matt worked in the Post Office to augment his income. Lucy kept her job in the bank and together they made out. Just barely.

Robert E. Peary died in February, 1920 at the age of sixty-four. He had been ill for a long time with pernicious anemia. Science, though now able to control the disease, has never found a cure. One thing research has discovered in common among all sufferers is a history of severe emotional shock.

Henson, who had not seen his commander since their return

from the Pole, sent a letter of condolence to the Peary family. It was acknowledged.

Except for the Eskimos who had disappeared back into their tribes, Henson was the sole survivor of the dash to the Pole, and it was inevitable that, with the passing years and the cooling of the Cook-Peary passions, increasing efforts should be made to obtain proper recognition for him.

Four times bills were presented in Congress to award him a pension (1926, 1936, 1938, and 1949) and four times the bills were bottled up in committee. His recognition was going to have to come in a less substantial manner.

From the first his greatest champion was Donald MacMillan. With his own increasing reputation as an explorer, and his eventual rank as a Rear Admiral, MacMillan raised an increasingly effective voice in demands for justice to Henson.

In a letter to Illinois Governor Henry Horner on May 14, 1938, MacMillan appealed for pressure on Washington to pass a bill honoring Henson. After reviewing Henson's Arctic career, he concluded:

The importance of the part played by Matthew A. Henson during those eighteen years of struggle against the elements of the North has never been recognized by our country, or by a single organization in the United States. Knowing that honors and medals have been bestowed and awarded to men in a similar line of work, men who have not accomplished one tenth the amount of work, it is very evident that there is one reason only why Henson has not be[en] honored—he is black.

I understand that every one of Byrd's men, even the cook, the boy who fed the dogs, men who never left the warm hut seven hundred miles from the [South] Pole, received a gold medal from Congress. Surely they must feel that this man [who] helped to bring such a great honor to his country should in some way be recognized.[67]

MacMillan was wrong. The Congress did *not* feel that Henson's contribution to the nation should be recognized and the bill never got out of committee.

Gradually MacMillan began to make some progress on the non-governmental level, however. In 1937 Henson was elected to full membership in the Explorers Club and Lowell Thomas chaired a special dinner in his honor. March of the following year saw Henson elected an honorary member of the Academy of Science and Art of Pittsburgh.

In 1944, thirty-five years after the event, Congress did respond to the pressure by striking off one medal honoring *all* the men of the Peary expedition: Marvin, MacMillan, Bartlett, Borup, Goodsell, and Henson. This was apparently done on the theory that one black man diluted by five whites made a sufficiently weak potion to be swallowed.

The following year all members of the expedition received the Navy Medal. Henson received his in a private ceremony in the office of a commander. And in March of 1948 MacMillan succeeded in having the Geographic Society of Chicago strike off a gold medal for Henson and give him a testimonial banquet. The officials of the society were then humiliated to find that when their guest of honor arrived, no hotel would rent him a room for the night and they had to scurry around to find private accommodations.

Each year as the anniversary of the discovery of the Pole came around, Matt's story reappeared in the newspapers and he was honored in various ways. In 1950, the forty-first anniversary, he was honored in military ceremonies in the Pentagon and received a salute from President Truman. In 1954 President Eisenhower received him in the White House, and then he went to Arlington Cemetery to place a wreath on Peary's grave. Dillard University in New Orleans named its new gymnasium and auditorium Henson Hall. A Matthew A. Henson grammar school was built on South Avers Avenue in Chicago. The sculptor John LeFarge made a bust of him and it was presented to the National Association for the Advancement of Colored People by W. Averell Harriman.

Sparked by Herbert Frisby, a reporter for the *Baltimore Afro-American*, the Negroes of Maryland undertook a successful drive to have their native son honored. On the fiftieth anniversary, Maryland Governor J. Millard Tawes declared April 6 "Matthew Henson Day." And two years later there was passed by the State Legislature and signed by Governor Tawes a bill to provide for the installation in the State House of a bronze tablet honoring Henson. This was done with elaborate ceremonies, the first memorial plaque in that Southern state to honor a Negro.

The tablet inscription read, in part: "Son of Maryland, exemplification of courage, fortitude and patriotism, whose valiant deeds of noble devotion under the command of Admiral Robert Edwin Peary, in pioneer arctic exploration and discovery, established everlasting prestige and glory for his State and Country . . . Matthew Alexander Henson, Co-discoverer of the North Pole . . ."[68]

From long years of having been completely ignored, Henson now was suddenly billed as "co-discoverer" with Peary. This was certainly a brand of political hyperbole. If Henson was co-discoverer, so were Ootah and Ooqueah and Seegloo and Egingwah. He might, with more truth, be hailed as an "assistant discoverer," but such language wouldn't have the rounded sound so dear to orators' hearts.

[XXIII]

The honors that came to Henson did not alter his life. They were spread over the forty-six years that elapsed between reaching the Pole and his death, and since none of them contained a grant of funds, he remained tied to modest and routine days. He seldom attended meetings of the Explorers Club because he could not afford the cost of the lunch.

He was seventy years old in 1937, and was forced to retire on a pension of $1,020 a year. He took care of the apartment while Lucy worked, and cooked the meals at night for her when she got home. He took long walks, no longer through the crisp, clean air of the Arctic, but through the fetid air of Harlem streets.

If he had been largely ignored by history, he was a celebrity in his neighborhood. Small boys ran after him in the streets, crying, "Matt, Matt, hi, Matt!" And as they circled him they looked with awe at his "whip thumb." The right thumb was twisted and deformed from years of snapping the long whip above the ear of the king dog. The boys were both fascinated and fearful, for it did not seem beyond possibility that he might suddenly produce a whip and snap it above them and drive them down the street, crying "Huk . . . huk!" They almost wished he would.

Lucy was a great clubwoman and a faithful churchgoer. Every

Sunday Matt accompanied her to the Abyssinian Baptist Church, demanding only that he be allowed to sit in a rear pew. He never could bring himself to sit entirely through a sermon delivered by the Reverend Adam Clayton Powell, and toward the end he would sneak out of the church and stand on the curb to watch the passing traffic. He would be there when the services ended and the ladies in their Sunday finery swept out to form an admiring circle around him. It was "Matt this," and "Matt that," and "Matt the other thing" until Lucy finally took firm possession of him and marched him home.

He didn't talk much about the Pole in the later days. He explained, "Folks soon got tired of the subject. I got tired of talking about myself, too." He was a kindly and cheerful man who had no need to brag, who attracted friends not because of his exploits but because of himself.

His health was remarkably good until the end. He had an operation for a hernia and recovered well. But soon after he developed pains in the prostate. He was a man both self-sufficient and poor, and he did what such men do: he got hold of a book on homeopathic medicine and began to treat himself. Lucy did not know of his agony until one day she came home and found him sitting in a tub full of hot medication; then she called the doctor.

He was operated on in St. Clare's Hospital and died two days later, on March 9, 1955. He was eighty-eight years old.

The newspapers editorially marked his passing. There were a number of attempts to assess the man and his contribution. It was pointed out that the Arctic has become central to the twentieth century, that the Polar Basin has become the new Mediterranean, the "middle sea" of the earth, and is being contended for by all the great powers. Science may soon be able to alter the temperature balance and convert cold regions into hospitable and productive ones capable of containing and feeding future generations. Peary and Henson opened this new frontier.

Peary no doubt saw much of this on the horizon of his times, but Henson's motives and goals were certainly more modest. He started out for adventure, then went on to prove that his race is

capable of endurance and achievement, and he wound up with love
—love of the Eskimos. And there is his lasting monument.

Today there are Eskimo legends about Miy Paluk that bring
warm smiles to brown faces. The old men hand the legends down
to the younger ones, and for a hunter to have known Henson in
person is to distinguish him forever. These old men tell a story
about Miy Paluk when he first came north and could speak no
more Eskimo than a baby. He led them on long marches and great
hunting expeditions, and whenever he wanted to bring them out
of their igloos and onto the trail for a long stretch of back-
breaking work, he would shout "Ahdoolo! Ahdoolo!" It was a
meaningless word, a word he had made up, and each time he used
it, the Eskimos would double up in gales of laughter. And they
would keep chuckling over it during the march, the word warming them, cheering them on, making their work easier.

The word became part of the Eskimos' vocabulary, passed on
from generation to generation. It still has no specific meaning, but
vaguely expresses hope and courage.

To create a word, especially such a word as "ahdoolo," seems
sufficient contribution for any man.

Notes

Noted here are documents on the *written* words of the principals. Dialogue is an elusive element and even the man who speaks it can hardly be trusted to remember it with accuracy the following day.

1. Eivind Astrup, *With Peary Near the Pole* (Pearson, London & Lippincott).
2. Robert E. Peary, *Northward over the Great Ice,* Vol. I (New York: Frederick A. Stokes Company, 1898).
3. Stefansson Collection, Baker Library, Dartmouth College, Hanover, New Hampshire.
4. *Northward over the Great Ice,* Vol. I
5. Shown author by Cook's daughter, Mrs. Helene Cook Vetter.
6. Matthew A. Henson, *A Negro Explorer at the North Pole* (New York: Frederick A. Stokes Company, 1912).
7. Josephine Diebitsch Peary, *My Arctic Journal* (Contemporary Publishing Company, 1893).
8. *Northward over the Great Ice,* Vol. I.
9. *Ibid.*
10. *Ibid.*
11. *Ibid.*
12. Shown author by Lee's son, H. Wales Lee.
13. *Ibid.*
14. *Northward over the Great Ice,* Vol. II.
15. *Ibid.*
16. *Ibid.*
17. *Ibid.*
18. *Ibid.*
19. Shown author by H. Wales Lee.
20. *Ibid.*

21. *Ibid.*
22. *Northward over the Great Ice*, Vol. II.
23. Shown author by H. Wales Lee.
24. *Ibid.*
25. *Northward over the Great Ice*, Vol. II.
26. Robert E. Peary, *Nearest the Pole* (New York: Doubleday Page & Company, 1907).
27. *Ibid.*
28. *Hampton's Magazine* (January, 1910).
29. Robert A. Bartlett, *The Log of Bob Bartlett* (New York: G. P. Putnam's Sons, 1928).
30. *Nearest the Pole.*
31. Letter to author from MacMillan.
32. *A Negro Explorer at the North Pole.*
33. Letter to author.
34. Robert E. Peary, *The North Pole* (New York: Frederick A. Stokes Company, 1910).
35. *The Log of Bob Bartlett.*
36. *The North Pole.*
37. *Ibid.*
38. *Ibid.*
39. Letter to the author.
40. George Borup, *A Tenderfoot with Peary* (New York: Frederick A. Stokes Company, 1911).
41. Letter to the author.
42. Donald B. MacMillan, *How Peary Reached the Pole* (Boston: Houghton Mifflin Company, 1953).
43. *The North Pole.*
44. *Ibid.*
45. *How Peary Reached the Pole.*
46. *Ibid.*
47. *A Tenderfoot with Peary.*
48. *The North Pole.*
49. *Ibid.*
50. *How Peary Reached the Pole.*
51. *Ibid.*
52. William Herbert Hobbs, *Peary* (New York: The Macmillan Company, 1936).

53. William A. Brady, *Showman* (New York: E. P. Dutton & Co., Inc., 1937).
54. *Ibid.*
55. J. Gordon Hayes, *Robert Edwin Peary* (London: Richards & Toulmin, 1929).
56. *The Log of Bob Bartlett.*
57. *A Tenderfoot with Peary.*
58. *How Peary Reached the Pole.*
59. Hobbs, *Peary.*
60. *Ibid.*
61. *Ibid.*
62. Shown the author by Marie Peary Stafford from the Peary family archives.
63. *Ibid.*
64. *Ibid.*
65. *A Negro Explorer at the North Pole.*
66. Peary family archives.
67. Shown author by Admiral MacMillan.
68. Shown author by Herbert Frisby.

Bibliography

ALLEN, EVERETT S. *Arctic Odyssey*. New York: Dodd, Mead & Co., 1962.

AMERICAN ASSOCIATION FOR THE ADVANCEMENT OF SCIENCE. "Engineering Features of the Nicaragua Canal." *Proceedings 36th Meeting* (New York, August, 1887). Pp. 174–78.

ANDREWS, ROY CHAPMAN. *Beyond Adventure*. New York: Duell, Sloan & Pearce, 1954.

ASTRUP, EIVIND. *With Peary Near the Pole*. Pearson, London & Lippincott.

BARTON, REBECCA C. *Witnesses for Freedom*. New York: Harper & Brothers, 1948.

BERENS, S. L. *Nansen in the Frozen World*. Philadelphia: Holman & Co., 1897.

BORUP, GEORGE. *A Tenderfoot with Peary*. New York: Frederick A. Stokes Co., 1911.

BRADY, WILLIAM A. *Showman*. New York: E. P. Dutton & Co., 1937.

BRIDGMAN, HERBERT L. "Peary, the Man and His Work." *Acts of the 10th International Congress of Geography* (Rome, 1913).

COOK, FREDERICK A. *My Attainment of the Pole*. Mitchell Kennerley.
———. *Return from the Pole*. Mitchell Kennerley.

DUTTON, COMMANDER BENJAMIN. *Navigation and Piloting*. Annapolis, Md.: U.S. Naval Institute, 1858.

"Engineering Features of the Nicaraguan Ship Canal." *Iron Age*, Vol. XL, No. 20 (November 17, 1887). P. 11.

FREEMAN, ANDREW A. *The Case for Doctor Cook*. New York: Coward-McCann, 1961.

FREUCHEN, PETER. *Arctic Adventure*. New York: Farrar & Rinehart, 1935.

[215]

GREELY, MAJOR GENERAL A. W. *Handbook of Arctic Discoveries*. Boston: Little, Brown & Co., 1907.

GREEN, FITZ-HUGH. *The Man Who Refused to Fail*. New York: G. P. Putnam's Sons, 1926.

HALL, THOMAS F. *Has the North Pole Been Discovered?* Boston: Richard Badger, 1917.

HARTLEY, HUGH H. "Admiral Peary Applies for His First Job," *U.S. Naval Institute Proceedings*, Vol. LXIII (June, 1937).

HAYES, J. GORDON. *The Conquest of the North Pole*. New York: The Macmillan Co., 1934.

————. *Robert Edwin Peary*. London: Richards & Toulmin, 1929.

HEILPRIN, ANGELO. *The Arctic Problem*. Contemporary Publishing Co., 1893.

HENSON, MATTHEW A. *A Negro Explorer at the North Pole*. New York: Frederick A. Stokes Co., 1912.

HOBBS, WILLIAM HERBERT. *Peary*. New York: The Macmillan Co., 1936.

HOPPIN, B. *A Diary, Peary Arctic Expedition of 1896*. New Haven, Conn.: Published by the Author, 1897.

HUGHES, LANGSTON. *Famous Negro Heroes of America*. New York: Dodd, Mead & Co., 1958.

KEELY, ROBERT and G. G. DAVIS. *In Arctic Seas, the Voyages of the Kite*. Edward Stern & Co., 1892.

LEWIS, CHARLES LEE. *Famous American Naval Officers*. Boston: Page & Co., 1924.

MACMILLAN, DONALD B. *Eskimo Place Names and Aid to Conversation*. U.S. Navy Hydrographic Office, 1943.

————. *How Peary Reached the Pole*. Boston: Houghton-Mifflin Co., 1934.

MARKHAM, SIR CLEMENTS R. *The Lands of Silence*. Cambridge: Cambridge University Press, 1921.

MITCHELL, HUGH C. "Peary at the North Pole." *U.S. Naval Institute Proceedings*, Vol. LXXXV (April, 1959).

MOUNTEVANS, EDWARD R. G. R. *Arctic Solitudes*. London: Lutterworth Press, 1953.

PEARY, JOSEPHINE DIEBITSCH. *My Arctic Journal*. Contemporary Publishing Co., 1893.

PEARY, ROBERT EDWIN. "Across Nicaragua with Transit and Machete." *National Geographic Magazine*, Vol. I, No. 4 (1889). Pp. 315–35.

————. "In Greely's Old Camp." *McClure's Magazine*, Vol. XIV (January, 1900).

————. "A Letter from Fort Conger." *National Geographic Magazine*, Vol. XII (October, 1901).

————. *Nearest the Pole*. New York: Doubleday, Page & Co., 1907.

————. *The North Pole*. New York: Frederick A. Stokes Co., 1910.

————. *Northward over the Great Ice*. Vols. I and II. New York: Frederick A. Stokes Co., 1898.

POND, J. B. *Eccentricities of Genius, Memories of Famous Men and Women of the Platform and Stage*. Dillingham Co., 1900.

"The Rio San Juan de Nicaragua." *Bulletin of the American Geographical Society*, Vol. XXI, No. 1 (March 31, 1889). Pp. 57–86.

ROBINSON, BRADLEY. *Dark Companion*. New York: Robert M. McBride & Co., 1947.

ROGERS, JOEL A. *The World's Great Men of Color*. Published by the Author, 1947.

SENN, NICHOLAS. *In the Heart of the Arctics*. Hammond, Ind.: W. B. Conkey Co., 1907.

STEFANSSON, VILHJALMAR. *The Friendly Arctic*. New York: The Macmillan Co., 1922.

WEEMS, JOHN E. *Race for the Pole*. New York: Henry Holt & Co., 1960.

Index